Simple and Silly Social -Cultural Strategies to Fight Isolation in Higher Education

Elizabeth Paradiso Urassa

Published by Information is Power, 2023.

Also by Elizabeth Paradiso Urassa

Strategies to Overcome Challenges in Academic Supervision
Simple and Silly Social -Cultural Strategies to Fight Isolation in Higher Education
Articulating Research Students' Relational and Social Expectations
The Academic Support Research Students Must Obtain from Supervisors
A Call for Inspection Unit for Research Students' Supervision

Table of Contents

Simple and Silly Social-Cultural Strategies to Fight Isolation in Higher Education

Dedication

This book is for higher education stakeholders, thus students, advisors, and supervisors. Likewise, the book is devoted to government officials, policymakers, donor agencies, and families who tirelessly support students in achieving their learning goals.

Definition of Terms

Culture Is a term that defines the values, norms, and social life activities of a particular group of people and that constructs and defines them differently from other groups.

Knowledge Is an understanding or awareness that originates from intuition, learning, observation, and experiences that lead to the acquisition of certain skills that support an individual in performing specific or general tasks.

Learning Is the process of acquiring new knowledge or modifying the current understanding, values, and skills through personal initiatives, friends, family, and experiences (informal) or a structured and organized learning system of schooling with the help of teachers, learning the curriculum and other learning agencies in a formal setting.

Learning agencies- This is a collection of individuals and supporters who facilitate an individual's learning in HE. It may be peers, friends, administrators, librarians, tutors, and family members. Online learning programs provided by most universities can be categorized among the learning agencies where students consult the programs for knowledge at their own pace.

Learning environment -Refers to learning in a natural setting where both learners.

and teachers meet physically. It can be in a classroom, laboratory, seminar, or workshop room, but the participants interact physically.

Online learning -occurs when the learner and the teacher use a device and a particular media program to communicate the learning contents without a physical setting and contact.

Stakeholders Is a generic term for all legitimate parties supporting HE students' learning process academically, socially, politically, and financially. These include institutional management, coordinators, students, advisors, parents/guardians, supervisors, employers, governments, and funding agencies.

Academic Refer to a university teacher or a scholar with qualifications recognized by HEIs, and who may carry supervision responsibilities for HE students. It also means the educational and learned person or a group. The term is used interchangeably with supervisor and faculty.

Parties Are social gatherings where students and others at universities socialize, enjoy, and get to know each other.

Ceremonies Are official assemblies that may include students and their learning agencies and are sometimes written in the University calendars

List of Tables

List of Figures

Introduction

There are many challenges facing higher education institutions and students today. Some of them are detected early by scholars and obtain the attention of institutional management and government before their development. Others are hidden and difficult to identify, sometimes ignored until they have caused regrettable damage to learners. For example, failure to cope and adjust to contextual social-cultural practices has become a stumbling block for many students leading to dropping out. However, little, and sometimes no, attention is directed to supporting students coping with contextual social-cultural practices, hence creating students' isolation problems.

Thus, if students' loneliness dominates most higher education institutions, as informed by scholars, it is time for students to obtain social guidance. The institution management should seriously inform students about the social-cultural values required and communicate the strategies to achieve them. Further, they must inform students of the effects of failing to cope with social-related aspects on their learning, especially in working with their learning agencies. Even though discussing social-relational aspects in multicultural learning environments is challenging, students should comprehend and practice vital contextual norms.

Indeed, scholarly literature has communicated the importance of mastering social aspects in learning and its importance in higher education students' integration. They have indicated that interaction with people in the learning community, acceptance of students' culture and as persons, and support for students to acquire a sense of belonging are the fundamental issues that bring success to students learning. However, some social aspects are hidden, so understanding them should be influenced by knowledgeable people. Indeed, it is time to support students because a lack of social-relational cultural skills has become a primary cause of students' failure to attain their degrees.

In many universities, students feel abandoned and remain in an isolated learning environment, especially doctoral students in humanity and art. These students normally deal with individual research projects that allow them to detach from each other and their learning agencies. Unfortunately, many students are affected by isolation and fail to communicate their challenges in coping with the situation, hence dropping out.

Indeed, little has been done to support students with practical information that may accelerate their integration. As a result, higher education students are unaware of the social-relational behavior required to succeed in contact with others and be part of the learning community. Therefore, this book aims to support students with reliable and practical information to help them comprehend the vital social skills required to integrate successfully. It provides a step-by-step process to cope with social-cultural learning environments in higher education anywhere. The book is a part of the book " The cultural qualities you must acquire to succeed in higher education," published in 2020.

I have received feedback from readers who wish to have extended information and portable books on all the topics separately. Previously, I included social, academic, and societal cultures that students should master to succeed in higher education in one book. One of the challenges the book readers have faced is carrying the heavy book with all three topics around. They also recommend more virtual figures for summary and points to remember. Therefore, separating the topics can allow readers to hold on to the paper book quickly and focus on one issue at a time.

The message in this book is one of its kind, discussing simple, silly, but vital social-cultural aspects and issues for higher education students to consider seriously. It attempts to guide students in dealing with fundamental relational issues and procedures to undertake in their learning environment. In addition, the author tries to narrate information from people willing to share their stories with readers for learning purposes. Such stories are vital in providing insights about higher education social situations that students must observe, learn, and practice correctly. I believe learning from others' experiences may lead to good teaching and an understanding of students' requirements in different social circumstances.

The structure of this book follows the table of content and one needs seven days to read the whole book. Of course, completing reading within a day is not challenging for good readers, but I recommend reading one chapter daily to spare time to digest the content. Thus, the readers should allow time to understand what they read, discuss, and analyze it with others. Likewise, readers should evaluate the content to determine whether it applies to their learning environment. Some issues may raise doubt, debate, and further investigation on the topic as they are partly the book's objectives.

The first chapter informs the scholarly discussion on student attrition and higher education learning cultural change. The second chapter focuses on globalization and cultural differences in higher education, where people have become mobile and borderless. In addition, the third and fourth chapters describe the culture of greeting people and its advantage in a new learning environment. Although demonstrating welcoming actions to others are the most neglected issues to discuss with students in higher education, the actions have the power to resolve many isolation challenges. Therefore, I emphasize the correct performance of greeting and demonstrate its benefits and how greeting may create integration and togetherness.

Furthermore, the fifth chapter discusses the smiling culture, which most people may be confused about when executed. I presume to categorize smiling into two styles, "I see you" and "I care for you," which convey different meanings. The benefits and magic of smiling are part of the discussion that students need to observe, learn, and practice. In addition, I provide some challenges associated with smiling, give precautions, and advise preserving the facial outlook of the participants. Indeed, smiling may convey the same meaning globally, thus, friendly, but the degree of friendship may be challenging to define.

Another issue in this discussion is the dress code for higher education students, discussed in chapter six. I emphasize professional dressing according to the event and context norms in higher education. Indeed, the dress code informs the learning community's norms and the student's values. So, observing it may be beneficial to avoid unnecessary misunderstandings, which may lead to isolation. Although I mention the liberty in dressing, sometimes it may lead to disadvantages if it is against the contextual dress norms.

Finally, I discuss the culture of ceremonies most students attend during their learning. Indeed, there is no way students complete higher education without attending parties, especially those learning in physical settings. Parties are the major tools for socialization, and most students are unaware of the social culture required.

I remind students of the cost-sharing culture of organizing parties to cover the expenses associated with the venue, music, and food or drinks. Students should seek adequate information about the party they desire to participate in and evaluate their budget to avoid embarrassment. I also remind students of the challenges parties may pose to their safety, especially those held outside the University's campuses. The discussion highlights the importance of surrounding themselves with reliable friends and being aware of their alcohol consumption limitations.

The book does not cover all areas of social-cultural issues students need to observe, but it reminds them to be attentive to the mentioned social-cultural issues to succeed in their integration to fight isolation. They must evaluate their learning social-cultural demands and strategize to fulfill them successfully. If one comprehends and practices the recommendations in this book, he can study anywhere globally without significant social-relational cultural challenges. Fortunately, as mentioned earlier, no one forces students to integrate into their learning community, but failing to comprehend and master social-relational cultural issues has become a stumbling block for many students. It is also one of the primary reasons for student attrition worldwide.

So, as a student, you must watch out.

Background Information

Scholars' information about the common cause of student attrition is in three categories: students' perception of themselves, changes in higher education structure and practices, and challenges in social-cultural practices. Surprisingly, in social-cultural practices, the failure of students to master and perform simple contextual, silly, and vital social actions is the reason behind students' isolation.

We may agree that the primary task of higher education institutions is to nurture and produce skilled laborers. The success of this significant task depends on how institutions effectively support students in remaining and completing their degrees. Unfortunately, several scholarly pieces of literature inform the challenges most HEIs encounter associated with student attrition and their hazards. The problem severely affects higher education (HE) stakeholders, thus, students, parents, institutions, donor agencies, governments, and teachers. However, little has been done to determine how social-relational cultural factors affect students learning and how to support students in acquiring the required social culture. Likewise, there is a lack of strategies to support students in overcoming cultural challenges in their learning environment.

Understandably, all societies that desire to develop socially, culturally, and economically require a competent workforce. Universities are known for their ability to construct and produce knowledgeable human resources with up-to-date and universally applicable knowledge and skills compared to other levels of formal education. Consequently, university graduates are regarded as skilled laborers for societal development and assumed to be able to solve various problems scientifically. Indeed, one may have a different opinion about this claim, but employers still encourage hiring jobseekers with a degree or more.

Therefore, universities and colleges ensure that the global community acquires skilled laborers. Unfortunately, it is considered a loss when students drop out of their studies, even when withdrawal occurs for a purpose. It is assumed that all students should complete their studies and acquire a degree as the ultimate learning goal. So, when counting student attrition as a loss, the most affected stakeholders are the students in question, institutions, and parents who typically invest in their children's education. Others equally endured the loss are governments, funding agencies, and the job market, which suffer a shortage of skilled laborers (if we still believe they come from universities and college graduates). Therefore, if we desire to observe students' graduations, it is time to support them in understanding vital social-relational cultural aspects they should master to remain in their studies, fight isolation, and graduate successfully.

According to diverse scholarly literature, the causes of student attrition are various. However, the dominant ones are associated with social-cultural aspects that students are ignorant of. Unfortunately, their unawareness remains even when some students dropouts as a sign of failure to cope with social-cultural practices. Indeed, the institutions' management fails to see the need to appropriately guide students on social issues, hindering them from integrating and developing a sense of belonging.

Unfortunately, this book cannot discuss all the reasons for student attrition due to its focus on social-relational cultural factors. However, one may follow the scholarly discussion about student attrition, multicultural, and the challenges they encounter in their learning by Ali, Kohun, & Levy (2007), Lee (2007), Manathunga (2005, 2007, 2009, 2014), Maher & Macallister (2013), Tinto (1987), Wisker (2005, 2012), Carter and Kumar (2017) and Grant (2005). Of course, many scholars have devoted their resources to informing the situations facing higher education students, and their writings can be beneficial in understanding the topic. It is also not the objective of this writing to list all key players and scholars who have written on the topic of attrition in higher education. Still, the mentioned scholars can provide the insight required to cope with the discussion in this book. You may also benefit by reading all the references listed on the last pages of this book.

In a net shell, scholars' common causes of student attrition are in three categories: first, students' perception of themselves and their ability to cope with changes in higher education learning. Second, their encounters related to failure to translate and practice appropriate contextual social-relational cultural behavior. As a result, such students find themselves getting into problems with their learning agencies and staying out of the institution and learning community norms. At the same time, they fail to communicate their weaknesses, needs, and expectations to the appropriate people. Third, the majority misconstrues their learning agencies' roles, responsibilities, and expectations, including their supervisors. Therefore, misperceptions, miscommunications, and misunderstandings create a gap between students and their learning agencies, hence isolation.

For the students to manage cultural change, they need reliable information and guidance to prepare them to face the reality of the current multicultural learning situation. Unfortunately, some HE students commence their studies without information about the institution's learning culture, structure, and practices. The lack of knowledge about higher education learning culture and their wrong perceptions of cultural expectations are significant hindrances. Such adverse experiences about learning culture and their position create failure in interaction with supporting agencies such as advisors, supervisors, and peers. As a result, some students experience cultural shock, which becomes the cause of withdrawal.

Attention is required to reduce and eradicate the problem by supporting students with social-cultural information. Indeed, adequate knowledge about higher education learning culture may help students prepare themselves, change their perceptions, and acquire strategies to cope and succeed. Most students' current illusive perceptions about the HE learning environment have brought several challenges. Many apply their previously acquired cultural practices, which influence students' insights and sometimes conflict with the new learning environment. Moreover, the culture may hinder their ability to cope with the current institutional norms. Cultural differences can also exist in departments and disciplines (science, humanities, and arts) within the same institution or community.

In most cases, some students who withdrew from HE perceived their cultural failure soon after enrolment and even before the formative and summative academic evaluations. In their new learning environment, such students experienced difficulties coping with many issues, such as the weather, food, and clothing. In many areas, others had problems working with their learning agencies, such as peers, advisors, and teachers. Others found it challenging to cope with teaching methods proposed by their teachers, primarily when they did not obtain answers to their questions related to learning culture. The disappointment may increase by the lack of shared expectations with the learning agencies regarding their roles and duties. Students often have different expectations of teachers' positions and responsibilities that differ significantly from the contextual reality.

Undoubtedly, students encounter many challenges in HEIs, leading to attrition. This crisis has no respect for institutions, nations, or continents, nor the type of degree, learning structure (online or physical settings), style (part-time and full-time), and practices. Scholars (Beer & Lawson, 2018) have researched this problem to determine the reasons for student attrition. They also desired to solve the problem through different research projects where students and other learning agencies participated in describing the challenges they faced. Indeed, students and their teachers are the main actors who can explain the matter and find a solution to the problem. Reading the scholars' publications may provide an understanding of the scope of the problem.

Undeniably, the magnitude of the cultural norms in higher education and how it affects students is unclear. Therefore, this book describes four significant social-related cultural practices one may consider and suggests strategies to combat the problem. Indeed, students who experience difficulties in the areas discussed in this book often find it disturbing to continue their studies. The situation hinders them from attaining their degrees regardless of whether other factors facilitate their learning.

Nevertheless, I must say that students who have failed to graduate are not always the losers because they might have withdrawn after acquiring vital knowledge and skills. Indeed, research training is a long process, specifically for doctoral students, and students may become resourceful even before graduation. So, I cannot undermine the achievement some students reach through their learning process, even if they do not attain the final goal of graduation. In my investigation of higher education learning, I always appreciate the views of graduates and non-graduates who have attended higher education for research degrees. Those who have attained their degrees are equally important as withdrawn because their views matter in bringing changes in higher education.

Therefore, this book reports diverse conversations with HE students, learning agencies, and the literature to help readers comprehend the situation. The information can support higher education stakeholders worldwide and hinder student attrition caused by cultural aspects. It might be challenging to stop a multicultural higher education learning environment movement, which has developed roots in many universities. So, coping with simple and silly social-cultural aspects that facilitate learning can benefit students and ensure the production of socially skilled laborers. So, the book's primary aim is to guide students to embrace the multicultural learning environment by learning contextual social-relational cultural practices. It also encourages students to perform appropriate contextual social culture in all areas of their learning to gain acceptance leading to integration.

Chapter 1

Scholarly Views on Student Attrition

Higher education institutions should emphasize creating a welcoming and inclusive learning environment for students of all backgrounds as a sustainable measure to reduce attrition.

Higher education student attrition is a problem facing many universities worldwide. It is a problem rooted in diverse challenges facing students, and sometimes they do not communicate with the right people for solutions. One of the problems mentioned by scholars is the change in the social-cultural aspects that expose them to unfamiliar norms. For example, according to Maher and Macallister (2013), in Australia, the Department of Education and Training, back in 2004, reported undergraduate attrition rates of 21.2% and 18.0% for domestic and international students, respectively. Likewise, Gabb, Milne, and Cao (2006) wrote that student attrition in one of the Australian universities from 1994 to 2003 was 25%. Similarly, O'Keeffe's (2013) study showed that HE student attrition rates reached 20% in Australian universities. Indeed, Australia is one of the countries with higher education multicultural learning environments representing others of the same kind.

Similarly, Golde (2000; 2005) argued that at least 40% of Ph.D. students withdraw from their studies each year in American postsecondary education. He also indicated some studies that estimated the attrition of doctoral students to be between 40% to 50%, whereas the undergraduate attrition rate was 10% to 20% at selective institutions. Also, O'Keefe (2013) indicated that the attrition for Ph.D. students was between 30% and 50% in the US. In another study, Mayo, Helms, and Codjoe (2004) learned that the retention rate in the University System of Georgia in 2011 was 59.8%, which aligns with what other scholars informed.

Johnes and McNabb (2004) reported that HE student attrition is a persisting challenge in the UK. The attrition rate raised from about 13% to 16% in the late 1970s and early 1980s to 19% to 25% in the 1990s. Likewise, Johnston (2005) in Becker and Becker (2008) (revealed that the University of Edinburgh, Leeds, London, Manchester, and Ulster had 22.0%, 8.6%, 11.0%, 8.6%, and 22.0% attrition rates in 2003-2004. In addition, Kettell (2018), when discussing young adult carers[1] applying the work of Sempik and Becker (2013, 2014), informed that 29% of students dropped out of their studies. So, the problem is reducing the number of graduates in the UK, calling for intervention.

According to the scholarly literature, several measures should be considered to fight against higher education institutions' student attrition challenge. For example, O'Keefe (2013), Maher and Macallister (2013), McMillan (2005), and Ali and Kohun (2007) suggested the increase students' learning resources by ensuring they receive adequate support to master social and academic aspects required of them. The second argument was to re-examine students living arrangements to create more comfortable living conditions with interactive learning facilities and situations. Third, they also proposed that students be restricted in employment because if students work exceedingly, it minimizes their chances of participating in social and academic activities. Fourth, scholars suggested changing pedagogical methodology and teaching structures to create a more inclusive learning environment that accommodates all students and helps them feel worthy, needed, and valued.

Other procedures mentioned by the scholars were to increase peer support, where students support each other in their group discussions and other available gatherings. The idea of peer support is not limited to students with their fellow students but expanded to other learning agencies such as advisors, librarians, and technicians. Moreover, faculty availability and accessibility to their students were essential factors for students' success. For example, scholars recommended that supervisors be available and accessible around the university campuses to allow informal interactions with their students. Likewise, innovative advising programs where students can obtain helpful information on their challenges are equally important. Likewise, students should be critical thinkers and share their concerns with the appropriate people aiming to solve them.

In addition, scholars noted a review of the first-year curriculum as a vital measure to ensure students' needs are known from the beginning. The scholars added that effective induction programs for newcomers receiving essential information on the required social matters are critical to prevent misunderstandings. Moreover, scholars mentioned that discussing and comprehending social students' expectations can solve several challenges. Likewise, understanding supervisors' and students' roles could support student retention, learning, and graduation. Finally, higher education institutions should emphasize creating a welcoming and inclusive learning environment for students from all backgrounds as a sustainable measure of integration. Of course, the mentioned recommendations are a few out of many which can help prevent student attrition.

Figure one provides a summary of the scholarly recommendations.

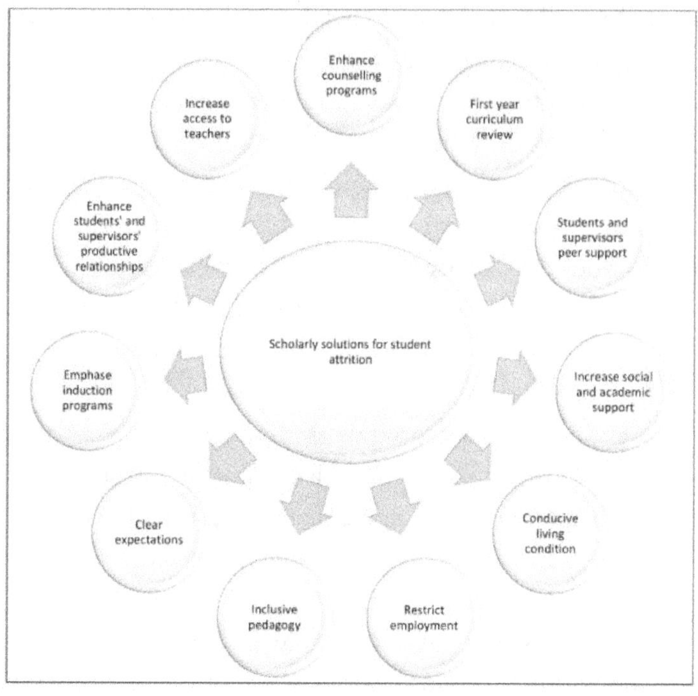

Figure 1. Scholarly Measures Against Student Attrition

According to figure one, the scholarly literature indicates eleven significant measures to fight student attrition. However, scholars did not reveal the specific contents of each proposal because institutional priorities vary, and contextual preferences should prevail. Likewise, academics did not explain how students should support themselves or obtain assistance from their learning agencies to reduce social challenges apart from supervisors' accessibility. They believed that if academics were accessible to their students, it might reduce attrition, but sometimes, they may be unapproachable. Another issue the scholarly literature cited was introducing and enhancing first-year induction programs. Again, they did not propose the information or content that might be useful for students to acquire in these initial programs.

Furthermore, scholars suggested changing the curriculum and increasing the counseling sessions to support students without indicating the appropriate content. It is assumed that each institution will cater to its needs and students' requests without uniformity. Another strategy was to improve higher education pedagogy to make it more inclusive, and again this recommendation depends on the contextual learning environment, whether homogenous or heterogenic. As a result, the approaches and programs' contents to support students are not uniform and may not universally apply if formulated.

Indeed, we must agree that the learning environments of most HEIs have changed, and the strategies for students' learning should also adjust accordingly. For example, some universities accommodate more international students than others, and few institutions have students from the same cultural background. Moreover, not all universities have adequate learning and teaching resources and students with different social and academic abilities. Therefore, institutions with varying contexts and resources should also have unequal social-relational cultural learning practices.

Additionally, Scholars discussed students' employment and excessive working hours as factors that accelerate attrition. Still, they did not indicate how students should solve financial challenges if they do not have a sponsor. Indeed, higher education costs are high, and not all students obtain financial support from reliable donors. Some may have limited funding contracts leading to financial uncertainty; sometimes, they should find a new sponsor each year. Such students need to work to secure their financial capability for their tuition, and the work reduces the time for their social activities accordingly.

Likewise, students learn under different expectations. For instance, the issue of excessive work can have various motives from one student to another. Some work because their communities expect material wealth rather than knowledge wealth in their return. The principle of expectations of material wealth may apply to host and international students depending on society's expectations. At the same time, others do not have such wealth-gaining and provision expectations or pressure on their students. Therefore, such diverging expectations of society may influence students' learning, and with the increase in wealth focus mindset, the growth of students' work ambition and maybe the cause of dropout. So, expectations factors are the fundamental aspects that lead to failure or success for most students and are rooted in culture.

In addition, academic literature indicates other causes of attrition, such as isolation, failure to cope with the learning environment, and students' perception of lack of support and belongings. But, again, most of the causes of student attrition are also rooted in students' cultural perceptions. It is also essential to remember that some students learn in a foreign environment even when learning in their country of origin. For example, one may join a university outside the birthplace within his country, hence foreign culture. It means that even if students come from the same continent or institution, they might have several new social-related cultural issues to learn about.

At the same time, HE's learning environment is different from high school, for those who join a bachelor's degree can experience shocking changes. For example, students who join second or third-degree in an institution distinct from the previous learning environment may also experience challenges when changing the learning environment, even within the same region. Likewise, various structures and practices inside the same university are observed based on departments and disciplines mandates. Such differences may be new and confusing to some students, and the experience may be challenging. The problem may increase significantly when the cultural practices differ greatly with a lack of guidance and if they are hard to accommodate.

Other scholars have mentioned the challenging relationship between students and their learning agencies, including supervisors, as the primary cause of student attrition. For example, Grant (2005) mentioned the crisis and chaotic situation in supervision where inequality between students and supervisors dominates. She compared the relationship between supervisors and students in some universities to that between slaves and masters. Her point is that the students receive orders, and the supervisors do not listen to students' needs and expectations. It is a pity because some supervisors do not even comprehend their students' needs, and no one monitors their practices with students. Indeed, Manathunga (2005) called for light on the supervision process, indicating the hazard of privacy in the relationship between students and supervisors. As a result, a lot happens in darkness, leading to student attrition, hence the call for attention.

Significant Solution

Indeed, according to academics, many factors are the sources of student attrition. Thus, it may be difficult to propose one solution for the diverse causes of the problem. However, I am taking a risk to offer a sustainable solution to the student attrition problem. I strongly believe in guiding students on social-relational cultural factors that scholars may have neglected. Focusing on cultural issues does not undermine other scholarly proposed solutions, but their suggestions may be successful if students perceive and master social-relational contextual cultural aspects. Cultural knowledge can help them tackle diverse challenges and understand themselves, their learning agencies, and their environment. I believe the ignorance concerning cultural issues and lack of proper guidance is the core of the student attrition problem.

Similarly, cultural factors are more critical than most HE stakeholders think. Unfortunately, most universities do not discuss cultural differences students encounter in their learning environment unless there are disputes. The institutions should allocate adequate time to deal with cultural issues and prepare programs to support their students. Although students are affected by cultural issues differently, and their reaction differs due to their diverse experiences, practices, and translations, guidance should be provided for them to succeed. Some can quickly cope with the changing situation because they can learn, filter, and practice what fits their learning environment. Others cannot accommodate cultural changes without adequate guidance, and in the absence of it, they withdraw from their studies.

I suppose it is time to provide students with relevant and adequate information concerning cultural issues. The prevailing culture must facilitate students' learning, not necessarily the students' used cultural norms. There is challenging to pick a specific context when discussing relational cultural practice due to the multicultural learning environment facing most higher education institutions today. So, students must comprehend the contextual and cultural qualities required and dominate their learning environment. It does not matter how comfortable the previous students' culture has been, but observing and mastering the contextual cultural practices may be more beneficial.

University students should obtain general information to help them strategize learning and acquiring the contexture culture. The student's success lies in their capability to efficiently merge into the departmental, institutional, and societal culture. Their integration ability is essential in determining the support other agencies can provide. In addition, learning about the contextual culture may help them better explain their needs and expectations and, in a manner, required than not knowing the culture.

The following section will highlight some higher education learning cultures that most institutions practice consciously and unconsciously. Indeed, it is the practice that almost all institutions accommodate and appreciates seeing in their students. Therefore, students who learn these practices correctly may cope with their learning environment more quickly than others. Besides, mastering the cultural aspects of greetings and smiling may be the initial door opener for many students.

Chapter 2

The Greetings Culture

How we greet people and our actions when greeting them, provide certain feelings that stay in their minds more extended than the topic we discuss. If that is the case, a greeting is a vital cultural aspect to learn for good social relations and integration.

The greeting culture is old, and each society has such a tradition to transmit to its offspring. So, people from diverse institutions may have different greeting habits based on their culture. However, the host institution and community greeting culture usually dominate previous students' culture. So, if this is the case, students should learn the contextual greeting culture properly and practice it for acceptance.

I want to share my encounter when undertaking degrees and how the greeting habit brought a special person to me. Initially, I was shocked by the greeting tradition because it diverged from my previous culture and needed some training. The main change was how people used body language, voice, and wording to express their feelings when they saw others. It was amazing but also shocking and unfamiliar; I felt confused, unsocial, and helpless. For example, people conveyed their greetings inversely, and the volume of their voices, interaction styles, and body language varied between and among them. One of the significant differences I observed immediately was the action and the reaction people demonstrated when greeting each other. It was an exotic action that met with a similar response; indeed, it differed from my previous greeting experiences.

I think the lack of exposure to other cultures before joining HE was one of the significant reasons for being so astonished by the new greeting norms. If I had observed multicultural greeting habits, the experience could have minimized the cultural shock I encountered in postsecondary. Unfortunately, when I studied in secondary school, social media was limited and not accessible to most people, including me. Besides, the available media focused on contextual events and information and little about people from other communities, hence the same tradition.

Indeed, we had two channels on the state-owned television and one company for national newspapers, which informed what the state desired. The government-controlled these sources of information, and the journalists wrote according to the wish of the government officials. Some executives had access to more information about global issues, including other cultures, than most people, and they were looked up to as a source of information. However, the state-owned media did not accept or allow anything out of the government's interest and something outside our definition of culture. There were no private-owned media for different information as it is today. Otherwise, I could have seen or heard of different cultural practices other societies were practicing, including the greeting style I met in the learning institution.

I originally came from a society where people greet each other quietly. Most of the time, the silence and quiet greeting were accompanied by intrinsic joy and respect without necessarily demonstrating it outwardly. People displayed happiness and excitement quietly and graciously without noise that could be noticed by those who were not part of the greeting. However, when I joined postsecondary studies for a bachelor's degree, it was my first time observing new greeting cultures. The learning environment had students from diverse backgrounds, and those outside the institution community were puzzled by greeting culture like mine. Therefore, we had to observe, learn, and imitate the contextual culture where applicable. The main issue was that the majority expressed their excitement openly when meeting and greeting each other. The process was active, vibrant, and exciting when people greeted each other, and I had no idea why people had to be so excited by just meeting someone else. However, I had determined to learn the meaning and perform the appropriate greeting style.

Initially, it was disturbing to cope with the new greeting culture. I thought it was an excessive exaggeration of the joy and pleasure of meeting someone, but in a real sense, it did not feel so. I had not seen people becoming erotic and hysteric when meeting others and shouting for nothing and everything. The most confusing was that the fun and excitement were not happening only between friends but to almost everybody in the institution's community. Indeed, the new greeting habit was glamorous and energetic but short-lasting. People's demonstration was always like something extraordinary had happened between and among them, and one could not believe it was just a mere greeting.

To describe it shortly, people made a big shouting of different kinds when greeting each other, such as Wahoo! Hi!!, Hello!!!! (Exaggerated style) How is Yooou? If someone started greeting by Wahoo!! Halloo!! How Are Yooou? The other person had to be excited with the same vibration and a BIG SMILE saying, Ohio, Halloo! I am very, very fine, thank Yooou!! (Exaggerated style) What about Yooou? If the other person said I miss you, the other could say I miss you very much. The excitement could be like a fire extinguisher after seconds or minutes, depending on their vibrations.

Initially, it seemed as if I were looking at one of the Hollywood, Bollywood, or Nollywood movies. I even lost my confidence in greeting people because I thought I lacked the required social qualities. Sometimes, I avoided meeting people and observed them practice the greeting culture from a distance. If not for the support I received from others in learning and training to greet properly, I could fall apart and abandoned my studies. So, I finally learned that the happiness of meeting people was strategic, calculated, and staged. The practice was strange because the joy and excitement disappeared soon after the greetings. Sometimes the participants could hug each other stylishly and move on as if nothing had happened. It was something I had not seen or practiced before, which disturbed me and brought a need to learn. Likewise, no one could explain why the greeting should be complicated and requires different manipulations. I did not even comprehend the meaning of all the exaggerations in the new greeting style. It was like a comedy show, and the practice was a big shock to me and others unfamiliar with the culture.

Indeed, people tend to think greeting others is a choice. It is not so all time; most people expect you to greet them, and you may desire to receive greetings from others. If you do not welcome people by greeting them, you may face isolation and other judgmental outlooks. So, in one way or the other, one has no choice but to take the opportunity to greet others correctly to avoid being sentenced as rude and selfish. In most societies, the greeting is the first command parents teach their children, and they create songs to remind children about this culture. When I was a little girl, my father, and mother said, "greet people even if they do not greet you back." This statement was the number one rule of interaction.

Unfortunately, I sometimes broke the commandment in the new learning environment in my bachelor's degree. I could not immediately change my smooth, careful, and observant greeting habit. Rather, I was embarrassed by how others behaved, and it was almost impossible for me to act the same. I was always cold and silent, altered a few words after greeting others, but lacked the excitement and joy others expressed. As a result, my greeting habit was boring, and I noticed that some students misunderstood me and my feelings because I had no pressure, fire, or vibration required for the new greeting style.

As I mentioned earlier, people change based on new perceptions and experiences. I realized later that some students who demonstrated excitement while greeting had acquired such behavior in the learning environment. However, most came from cultures without such noisy greetings (sorry for that), and they encountered some social challenges that made them change. Some explained that they desired to be part of the learning society, so they had to acquire a new culture.

Others said they found the unique greeting style exciting and suitable for interacting with others. Some of these students came from societies where people greet quickly with a few words, such as Hi! And the receiver would respond the same way, Hi! No one bothered to ask how the other person was or expressed excitement. They had nothing to add in their greeting except "Hi" unless someone intended to converse with the other person (s) or had a question.

The willingness to adapt to a new culture is vital but debatable. The integration may happen after one tries to understand why people act as they do. For example, some students changed their greeting style from their previous culture due to isolation in their new learning environments. They evaluated the reasons behind their loneliness and why other students had no time with them. They found that the proper greeting style was vital for them to catch on with people, obtain critical dialogue, and even build friendships. Some changed their greeting culture to attract people and be part of the learning society. Others changed to camouflage their differences and desired to be like anybody else. One of my informants, Jesse, who appreciated my calm greeting behavior, could not answer my question when I asked her why someone should yell like that while greeting. Instead, she said, "believe me, you will change soon." Indeed, as I mentioned earlier, some thought I was boring and unhappy when seeing others. They thought I was cold, unhappy, and unsocial, but few guys liked my contentment of quietness and politeness.

Indeed, the surroundings influence peoples' behavior. So, I had to learn the new culture to fit in the learning environment because I wanted to be part of society. Besides, it was harmless to be excited when seeing others and receiving their greetings. Nevertheless, I investigated the new greeting behavior and examined the reasons behind the greeting style and its benefits. I discovered that the new culture benefits the giver and recipient of the greetings. One of the significant advantages I found crucial and fascinating is the power of joy and positive energy transmitted during the greeting. People surrounded themselves with positive energy, which other performances could not bring.

Therefore, it was not the issue of wording or body manipulation but the power and joy involved. After I acquired some information about the new culture, I gradually modified some of the elements of my greeting style by becoming more active, lively, and welcoming when greeting. As a result, I became more dynamic and enthusiastic when seeing others and conversing with them. I noticed that my change in greeting attitude and practice made me happier. However, although I expressed more joy, excitement, and happiness, I did not acquire the shouting part of the new greeting habit. Therefore, my learning and adjustment allowed people to approach me easily and share my joy, energy, and excitement more than before.

Greeting, for some people, is not something to learn. Many assume they can greet without observation, guidance, or understanding from the context's point of view. But indeed, learning and acquiring the proper greeting habit, including executing it acceptably, is vital. As a reader of this book, you may think they do not need to learn to greet people appropriately. You think you have known how to greet people since you were a baby and that the HE learning environment will not be challenging. But, trust me, if you are unfamiliar with societal norms and greeting culture, you better learn it before enrollment. It is not OKAY to make mistakes when greeting people, especially from another culture, because it may provide an ill feeling. So, you must investigate how people salute in your learning community and how they respond to each other on different occasions and practices.

There are differences in greeting cultures in most learning institutions. Students and other learning agencies might have different greetings styles, but they must observe the culture in the learning context. For example, people might demonstrate happiness and joy when greeting each other in different ways, following specific rules or wording, while the body indicates friendly while greeting. Sometimes, there might be some gender-related greeting culture or religion-based greetings. For instance, some religious believers do not receive a handshake from individuals of the opposite sex. It is essential to understand the greeting style in advance to avoid being embarrassed by the rejection from people of the opposite sex. It may give you unnecessary ill thinking, mainly if the denial occurs publicly with your hand hanging to reach the hand of the other person.

Greeting habits are different and sometimes demonstrate peoples' positions. For example, some people bend their knees as a sign of respect for others with senior positions in their families or society. I believe this expression of bending the knees can mean something other than respect for different people. For example, in some cultures, all women bend their knees when they greet men, even a small male child. I am unsure whether this is connected to gender biases, respect, or humiliation, but most women deliberately execute such greetings. In some cultures, females bend their knees when greeting monarchy members, politicians, and religious leaders of both genders.

In most cases, the greeting style depends on the age and seniority of the participants. But, as I said, greeting culture is inherited, and one learns from childhood and most of the time without a good explanation. So, children may bend their knees when greeting their parents and other older people according to the cultural demand blindly. For example, bending the knees is connected to respect in most societies regardless of the participants' relationship. Presumably, Queens and Kings are the most recipients of such greetings globally. I suppose the people who bend to them acknowledge their majesty's seniority and display their modesty, but this is my subjective translation, which may differ from most practitioners. Overall, the knees' bending has the propensity to be associated with showing respect to the recipient.

Another person who receives such a knee bend greeting from women is the Pope of the Roman Catholic church. Even though Pope is not in a permanent position, they all receive respect due to their position. Most females do not stand still when greeting the Pope but bend their knees to demonstrate respect to the man of God. Others put one hand on the other while kneeling to Pope and those they respect. Christianity and churchgoers understand and obey the greeting principle as part of the rules. Sometimes they alter some words accompanying their knee-bending greeting actions, such as praise Lord, Haleluya, God is good, and the like.

However, if I generalize the bending of the knees as a sign of respect, I might be biased. I do not think all who bend to others always think of demonstrating anything than attending the culture. It might be that some people knee without such a kind of submissive thought, and they find themselves acting automatically. Sometimes they do not even acknowledge the seniority of those they greet; instead, such people practice what they have learned from childhood. However, most have been practicing such greeting culture for ages and inherited it from their parents and the previous generation. No one can tell precisely why it is like that and how it started, but it is a norm, standard, and quality regarded as appropriate to certain people and on specific occasions. So, if you are new to such cultural practice, you may think it is a deliberate action, and maybe you must not perform it, but in a real sense, you are obliged to act just in the same manner and perform it correctly. If you do not demonstrate greeting accurately and greet people the way they expect, you may create unforgettable and sometimes regrettable misunderstandings.

Likewise, men demonstrate different greeting styles to people they respect. Men are not normally bending their knees when exhibiting submissiveness or respect for others. Instead, most men express concern by removing their caps or leaning their bodies forward. As a male student, you may create a controversial situation if you greet someone you respect by bending your knee because it is not a gentlemen's style. On the other hand, if you lean your body forward and do not cover your head, it may demonstrate your consideration and respect for the recipient. Sometimes, when two or more male individuals meet, they can remove their caps as a sign of respect. However, some prefer shaking hands while standing straight without bending their bodies or knees.

Even though people usually attend to their culture by greeting, the correct salutations are vital. Yes, some people execute greetings without much thought about respecting the other person or the person's position. Indeed, proper practice indicates that the practitioner is respectful and obeys the required greeting culture even without the person telling him about that. So, it is vital to pay special attention when executing a greeting to other people around you. No matter what the intention is, whether you attend to the requirement of the culture involved or you mean to demonstrate respect to the person, the most important is the correctness of the act. Therefore, observing the greeting culture and training to acquire what you think can position you on the side of togetherness is essential. No one will sympathize with you for an incorrect greeting simply because you are from another culture. People expect the correct greeting style from those who dare to greet them, but if you cannot act appropriately, do not bother to greet people. You can pretend you have not seen them or are busy rather than executing an inappropriate greeting that may lead to misunderstandings. Indeed, learning to greet people correctly is not as costly as performing the act inaccurately.

Disadvantages of Incorrect Greetings

There are several disadvantages to an inappropriate greeting that no one desires. First, it shows the executor's unseriousness by ridiculing other peoples' cultures. So, learning and practicing the greeting act is vital to avoid misinterpreting one's behavior. Second, even if a person is genuinely stupid and lazy to learn about new cultures, it may be interpreted differently, which may withdraw favor that could be provided. Indeed, making a mistake when greeting people, especially those key players in the learning environment, can be a disaster. Third, it may create misunderstandings between the executor and the individuals who receive the greeting, often confusing the response. Folks may even think the executor is abusing their greeting culture and that the person mocks the traditions they respect.

So, although most do not think learning a new greeting style can be tricky, I think it is vital. It is easier for people to forget the mistake they make in solving mathematical algebra equations than the error in social relations, including greetings. Thus, the difficulties associated with the diversity in HE population may affect the greeting culture. So the differences are normal and should be communicated, and the learners of the culture should know irritable mistakes to avoid. The more they know how sensitive people are about their culture, the cleverer they become in learning and performing the act correctly.

However, some greeting styles can be uniform regardless of context. Others may be similar for all ages, gender, and seniority, even though some elements may differ slightly. For instance, one may understand the word and body posture when conveying and receiving greetings but fail to demonstrate the right attitude. One may need to show off gladness and optimism in meeting others and let go of a depressive attitude. So, in such a case, if you do not demonstrate a positive attitude, people may think you are not interested in them, or you are a slow learner if you cannot execute greetings with the right ingredients. They may even conclude that you will have significant challenges learning other disciplinary and professional issues if the greeting is challenging. It is also a negative impression of not desiring to be part of the host community, and maybe you need a space. Your weakness in saluting people may lead others to conclude that you want to be left alone. The situation can create discrimination and isolation that may cause you to feel uncomfortable and even drop out of your studies.

Moreover, incorrect greetings can also chase people away. As a foreigner and student, if you do not perform greeting action correctly, it may be a sign of disinterest in your host's culture. In return, people may not be friendly and attractive to you, hindering your integration. Therefore, as soon as you observe the lack of greeting culture as an obstacle to learning, it would help if you considered learning it seriously. When you have decided to learn the greeting style, perform the exercises in a private arena to obtain feedback before in public. If you practice in public and make mistakes when greeting folks, it may appear as if you are making jokes, and the response you obtain may even scare you. Making fun of other people's greeting habits can harm your relationship, and their reactions may not favor you.

If you consider not learning the greeting culture because you cannot observe its importance, it is well and good. However, do not complain when people forsake you and stop interacting. As I mentioned, you may become lonely and isolated without anyone to interact with if a simple or complicated greeting act is of no concern to you. If you do not demonstrate an interest in others and learn a new culture appropriately, people may also think you are conservative and against learning about others' cultures. In most cases, current higher education folks come from different areas, and students should be flexible enough to adjust to different cultures. Some may think you are proud of your culture and wish them to change for you rather than appreciating contextual cultures. Others may have different thoughts that may hinder one's integration.

Learning how to greet people in your learning environment is an essential tool for integration. If you do not absorb the culture of welcoming and saluting people correctly, you may continue being a foreigner for a long time. There are several disadvantages of remaining a foreigner in your learning environment. Some disadvantages are that you will not enjoy the local events around you and will not receive the loyal interaction as those who have integrated into the community. It can also be challenging to influence others with your ideas if you cannot become one of them through proper greeting traditions. In most cases, greetings create friendship and conversation, and many people have known each other and become lifelong friends through the greeting they provide to each other.

Indeed, an incorrect greeting can create distance and misunderstanding. This confusion is not only for host individuals but even for strangers. As mentioned, other people who receive greeting styles differently from expected can be disturbed in many ways. The greeting act is among the numerous essential practices humans observe when they meet for the first time. The way we greet people and the actions and attitude we execute when greeting provide certain feelings that stay in their minds more extended than the topic we discuss. So, dare to learn the correct greeting substances and styles in your learning community and execute it properly.

We can remind ourselves of the element of greetings in Figure two.

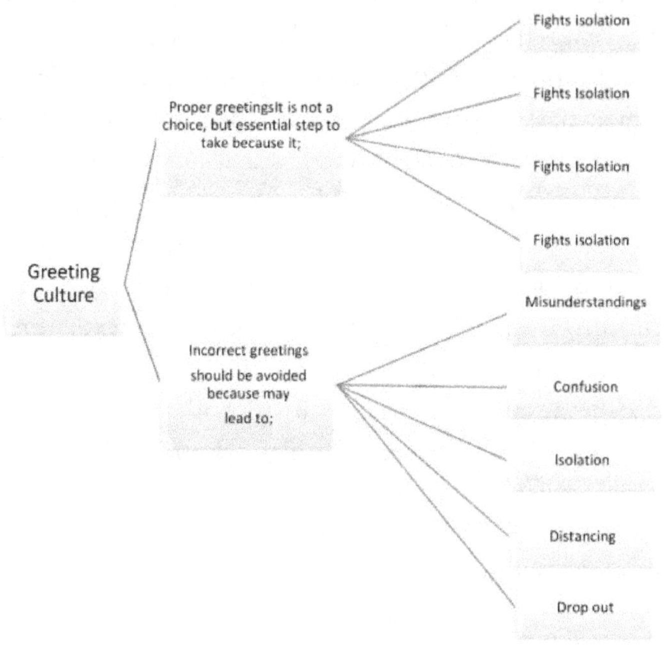

Figure 2. Greeting Culture and its Consequences

Correct greetings have various advantages, but if you remember the one in figure two, it might motivate you to learn and practice anywhere. First, remember that learning a new culture of greeting is not a choice but essential if you want to be part of the learning society. It is vital because it is a key to fighting isolation. After all, no conversation, relationship, or friendship happens without a greeting. After knowing this principle, you must believe that by executing correct greetings, you will open the closed doors of opportunities, and people will draw closer to you, hence no isolation.

Moreover, learning and practicing greeting culture demonstrate your respect and interest, which may build friendships and fight isolation. However, suppose you do not take greetings seriously, execute improper greeting styles, and demonstrate inappropriate attitudes and actions. In that case, you may bring misunderstandings that may end in confusion for yourself and others. In addition, you may disgrace yourself with distance from other people, including learning agencies, hence isolation. You know the next step following isolation; thus, drop out. So, learn and acquire proper contextual greeting culture to fight isolation.

The next chapter will discuss the advantages of learning and practicing contextual greetings properly. First, however, I want to share a greeting episode that can help students see the need to learn contextual greeting culture to avoid misunderstandings.

Chapter 3

A Greeting Episode

*R*e-examining *the greeting culture in a new learning environment is vital because, in some cultures, it is not a usual act not to greet whirls in others; it is not typical to greet unfamiliar people.*

Most of the time, people encounter different challenges when they meet with a foreign culture. Unfortunately, students can obtain guidance on other areas of social norms, but greeting is the most neglected part of orientation. For example, their advisors inform students about many issues in orientation programs except greetings norms. Mostly, they are topics that the university needs them to observe, understand and learn to comply with institutional and departmental rules and regulations, but not greeting norms. Even when it is evident that isolation is a major challenge in higher education, students still do not obtain guidance that can help them avoid it. So, the lesson about greeting practices is absent in many universities, and students drop out every semester partly because of isolation. Indeed, the consequences of mistakes students perform when greeting others in their learning environments may lead to long-lasting problems, if not attrition.

Therefore, I want to share the episode concerns greeting misunderstanding as one of my informants, Jane, consented. Although there are many details from a female first-year doctoral student about greeting culture in this narrative, I will inform only the part she allowed me to share. Her story is one of the stimuli and a catalyst for me to discuss the greeting issue in this book. The aim is to support students in higher education to observe, learn, and practice the contextual greeting culture appropriately. The story began on the first day she reported to a new university.

Jane was a new student in a foreign learning institution with a different greeting culture from the current one. The first day she arrived at the university campus, a man who introduced himself as an accommodation manager received her warmly. The manager hugged and held her near for a minute or two to express his joy and excitement. He also extended his greeting by asking her some questions in a friendly manner while working toward the students' residential compound. Finally, the manager expressed his generosity and gentlemanly behavior by opening the door for her, taking her bags to the shared living room, helping her off her jacket, and more talk. After their extended conversation, the manager continued his day, confusing the female student.

All that Jane experienced in that moment of greeting was contrary to her culture. The student experienced the greeting that only couples in her tradition could perform to each other. So, a man could not perform what the accommodation manager did if he was not thinking of being a partner or in love with her. The actions like hugging her, helping her with "unjacketed," taking her baggage, and asking her questions that the student regarded as private happen only to lovers in her tradition.

Indeed, the kind of questions and friendly interaction was unique and confused her completely. According to Jane's culture, some of the manager's questions were intimate; for instance, he asked whether her boyfriend was sorry for her to study abroad, and she was not expecting to be asked such questions by someone she had just met. She had no boyfriend and said so to the accommodation manager, who showed they were in the same boat. She was mystified, embarrassed, and thrilled by the queries and friendly atmosphere the manager created. She was bewildered, mixed with the shame and joy of being accepted and received in a friendly manner in the foreign learning environment. It was the most pleasant but confusing moment, and Jane thought maybe it was love at first sight.

Indeed, greeting culture can create uncertainty if not correctly executed and translated. Jane's comfortable greeting zone was disturbed, and she could not sleep that day, thinking the manager was in love with her. Jane was a beautiful single female student around twenty-five years of age who had no difficulty attracting anyone. According to her external appearance and attractiveness, one could say that Jane could choose a partner across cultures with minimal or no challenge, especially these days when a person's character is of little value to many. So, she thought, "of course, a manager is a handsome man; I am a beautiful lady; what is next, and how wonderful it is to be loved so quickly in a foreign region." She believed life would be simple in a foreign land with the manager beside her.

The whole night was disturbed, and Jane even planned what her wedding with the manager would look like. The doctoral student was terrified that it may interfere with her studies, and she thought of strategies to balance love and studies. But, simultaneously, she encouraged herself that everything would be all right and that she could ask for advice if she felt overwhelmed. Jane extended her thoughts to the wedding guests and how it would be exciting for her to get married. The student also thought of how wonderful it would be to introduce the manager to her community and stay partly in these two societies.

Not everything excited Jane when she considered being part of the foreign community. The female student felt miserable and disappointed because staying in a foreign country with the manager would disturb other plans. She did not like staying in a foreign land due to what she had invested in her country and her career position. Jane was a school of medicine head in her country of origin who had many people under her leadership. She obtained full sponsorship to develop her medicine and pharmaceutical leadership skills. If she remained in a foreign country, the student thought life would not be the same, especially for her career.

Jane thought about her family's disappointment if she stayed in a foreign country with the accommodation manager. The most disturbing issue was breaking her closeness with her mother and friends. She also thought marrying a foreigner could meet opposition from her associates, including family and friends. Although Jane thought her mother liked children and the concept of marriage would bring what her mother wanted, she was skeptical. Besides, having children in a foreign country would lead to other challenges, such as family baby care, and Jane's mother would miss them dearly. In addition,

Jane's mother was good at making delicious food and baking cakes, so Jane could imagine how her children would miss their grandmother's cakes and good food. This part brought doubt on whether to continue interacting with the accommodation manager or forsake all the plans.

Jane utilized the whole night planning an elusive future life with the accommodation manager. The misunderstanding and false interpretation of the manager's greeting style and a little conversation created the illusion, contradicting the students' greeting culture. The manager was unaware of the student's greeting culture limitations and translation. These two individuals' cultures differed, but Jane became vulnerable by accepting to mistranslate the new culture before learning its interpretation. It also seems that the student failed to set boundaries for thoughts. When responding to the manager's (so-called) private questions, she did not inform her limitation and privacy issues. Jane allowed the man to bridge her cultural norms, so the manager asked confusing questions. Her failure to openness cost her sleep the whole night and the elusive planning for an unrealistic future with the students' accommodation manager.

Indeed, one needs to be on the watch for cultural differences. Jane was excited and prepared for another good day to extend her interaction with the manager the following day. The new female student was happy, excited, and smartly dressed, ready to meet the man again. She did not see him for the whole day and was disappointed but hoped to see him the following day. Certainly, on the third day, all new students were expected to fetch residence keys for their cupboards; it was an opportunity to ask some questions, if they had, to the same leader. So, Jane was thrilled and planned to receive more attention from the manager. She had scheduled several issues to discuss with him if he would show interest. Like the other students, Jane went to the manager's office and waited for her turn.

Culture can be practiced automatically without much thought. While Jane was waiting outside the manager's office with others, the manager received information that a new student was waiting for him at the reception desk. The hardworking university man quickly went to the reception, hugged the new student like Jane, and posed extended questions, and the warm conversation continued. The student was also excited and happy in the conversation and asked the manager some exciting questions. Jane oversaw them and attempted to grasp some of the manager's questions to the other student. The discussion was alive as both were excited and enjoyed the company. Then, the manager and the new student went together to the residence compound as he did to Jane; he spent some time conversing with the student and probably performed similar generosity in assisting the students and making sure everything was okay as he did with Jane. After some time, the manager returned to his office, where some students, including Jane, were still waiting for him.

The manager did not pay attention to Jane as a person or to other students; instead, he read the names and provided them with the keys to their book cupboards and the information required. Jane took the time to observe his actions toward other students, and she finally realized that the man was genuinely and equally happy and excited for all students. Ultimately, the female doctoral student grasped that the manager was doing his job, and all the performances were part of fulfilling his duty in a manner aligned with the institutional culture. The warmth and the character he played were part of his job to make all students feel special and welcomed without other personal intentions. This observation was new to Jane and helped her learn the first vital greeting and generosity cultural lesson.

Jane also observed peoples' interaction in society and learned that the first meetings with people were consequential and special. People displayed generosity and warmth, a kind of contact, mostly when they met for the first time. They had a culture of believing that first impressions mattered to people and that foreigners were the groups that society provided comfortable feelings and welcoming actions. So, being a foreigner, Jane and other international students received the best welcome to make them feel at home. With this understanding, she finally dropped all the thoughts of love she had carried with her at first sight. She was somewhat motivated to learn other cultural elements and asked for the correct translation. Finally, the female student managed to master cultural qualities and even married another person from the same learning environment.

The Benefit of Proper Greeting

There are benefits associated with greeting people correctly. The appropriate greeting can open many opportunities, especially in a new environment and learning niche. Often, greetings provide the first impression when people meet for the first time, as they did to Jane and other students attended by the accommodation manager. It informs how careful one is with his actions and can make people draw closer or away from the person. So, the appropriate greeting measures can even attract people to learn from the executor if he has any knowledge to share. Unfortunately, some people's ideas have failed to penetrate the right minds because they could not pass the greeting test. It may be impossible to share knowledge with people one cannot greet properly, even when the information is essential and valuable.

Generally, a proper greeting demonstrates how respectful one is in Figure Two. For students who manage to execute the greeting act appropriately in their learning context, their actions display admiration. Besides, it indicates a willingness to learn and be vulnerable or positively allow other cultures to be part of them. Ultimately, the more a student shows interest in people and their culture, the more folks around them appreciate and mind their well-being. Indeed, studying in a foreign environment has not been easy for some students, but learning the culture, including greeting, can streamline the process.

By asking questions, learning from other people's experiences can be more beneficial than mere observation. Some are willing to share their mistakes to help others learn from them to avoid falling into a similar trap of cultural ignorance. For this reason, I may share another story of a lady named Monica to help someone know how to learn and practice appropriate social culture. Monica lived near the University where I studied for one of my degrees, and I will not forget her story. On the first day, I met her at a religious gathering, and she was introduced to me by a friend. Fortunately, I had learned some greeting cultural elements of the new learning society, and I saluted her correctly, just as indigenous. Monica was excited about my greeting practice, and she was attracted to me as a person from that day.

Therefore, every Sunday I went to the religious meeting, she could come to me to greet me and find out how I was doing with my studies. Surprisingly, she invited my friends and me to her home for dinner one Easter Sunday when she learned we would not go to our countries for the Easter break. Monica prepared the Easter ceremony like the "last super" Christian religious books discussed between Jesus and his disciples. Everything was perfect, including decorations, seating arrangements, wine, bread, and other food.

The elderly lady was generous and had few friends. So, she was also hungry for friends who could fight isolation and boredom in her life. Indeed, she was good at creating and maintaining friendships with new people; we have become friends today. Likewise, she supported me in learning the contextual and cultural aspects by providing relevant information and translations. I have since been her friend, and even after completing my studies, I invited her to my country of origin, where she stayed for ten days.

Our bond started with the correct greeting I executed when I met her for the first time, nothing else. I was unaware of how powerful the act was because it was customary to learn the greeting habit of people I desired in advance, no matter how difficult that may be. However, Monica disclosed to me after our bond developed that my greeting act and correctness were so welcoming that she could not resist the attraction. I also support her statement that the correct greeting from a foreigner can break a strong wall in peoples' hearts. Therefore, I encourage all students to care for correct greeting habits as a key to many opportunities in their learning environments.

Mastering a foreign greeting can also demonstrate how flexible one is. It might be difficult to perform the necessary actions without learning the tricks. When one executes the correct greeting style in an unfamiliar environment, the person appreciates society's culture. Moreover, it makes people admire the flexibility and prompt learning habit. It is essential to learn this because it is easy for many to ignore greeting culture, so if a student demonstrates the correct action of greeting, she may seem as exceptional. There will be some people to appreciate her behavior. Besides, it shows that the student seeks to be part of the learning community. Nothing brings people together than the greeting actions executed correctly by a new person in the circle or community. Refer to my story with Monica.

Another advantage of the correct greeting is that it minimizes the gap between foreigners and indigenous. When I learned the proper greeting in my learning environment, I was attracted to learning other cultural elements and acting like the people of the land. I did not want people to define me as rigid but flexible and accommodating. Besides, my appearance showed that I was not from the community; they knew even if I greeted people correctly and performed other cultural practices. So, it was not that I was covering my origin, as many may think; instead, I appreciated the new culture. Some students become rigid, thinking that adapting to another culture will make them seen as if they denied their previous culture. For students to observe, learn, and acquire multicultural practices, executing each of them where required is not negative. Of course, I desired not to be sorted and left alone; I was fighting isolation, so learning cultural elements saved the purpose.

Moreover, I became familiar with other cultural aspects that reduced the distance between others and myself. My greeting actions catalyzed my quick integration into the learning environment, where I was allowed to be part of the student advising committee after graduation. So, greeting became the most influential act in my learning.

Consequently, as mentioned, the correct greetings may cover the identity of being "a foreigner" that most students bare when studying abroad. Acceptable greetings style brings togetherness and cooperation with others from across cultures quickly. It creates a friendly atmosphere and calms the tension the individual differences could create. Further, it sometimes allows unexpected conversations with the recipients, just as the indigenous greet each other and asks about their well-being. In most cases, proper greetings tend to bring about inclusion and may lead to participation in learning community activities, opening more associations with contextual people.

Greeting people the right way can be even more critical for students in HE to attract appropriate associates. Students must have people around to guide them concerning the institution and society's culture. Moreover, for students to comprehend cultural issues, they need academic and non-academic advisors, and the best way to attract such persons is through greetings. Indeed, correct greetings may keep students close to individuals who may be vital to their learning, field, and other opportunities.

I must admit that before I met Monica, one academic had said, "In this society (where I was studying for a master's degree), people are sensitive to greeting habits. So, try to learn how to greet people around you correctly because it is not normal to pass by someone without greeting if you desire to create a friendly atmosphere. However, if you do not understand how to greet people based on their preferences and seniority, do not greet them. Pretending you did not see them or moving away is better." I did not initially understand him, but later I realized what he meant. Although I had a habit of learning the greeting act of people, I could not be focused on it as I did if not for his alert. Maybe I could think, "Hi, it is just a greeting, and I can greet people," but his emphasis was a catalyst for me to learn and realize the importance of greetings. As a result, I complied with the greeting culture of my learning agencies and everybody around me without exclusion. Therefore, with all those correct greetings brought to me, without a doubt, I finally understood what the teacher said was right. So, it is the same principle I want students and readers of this book to remember and practice; thus, greet people correctly or do NOT perform a greeting act.

In summary, proper greetings have different benefits, as indicated in figure three.

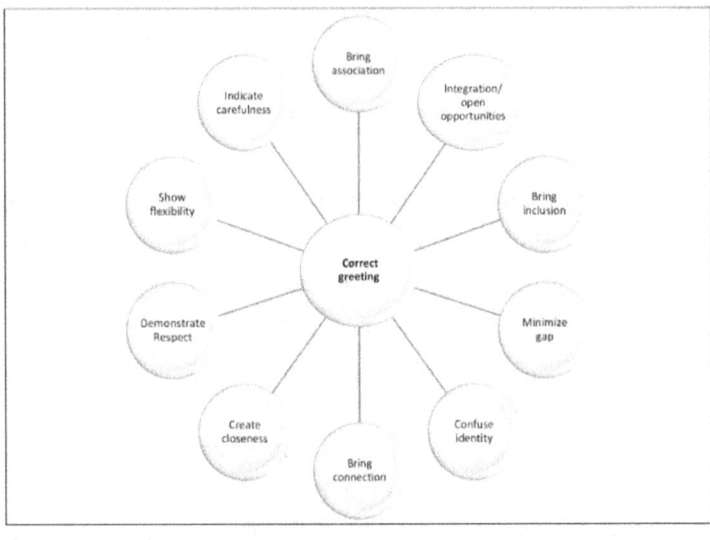

FIGURE 3. THE BENEFITS of Appropriate Greeting

In summary, the figure indicates some benefits of the correct greeting. Among the benefits are those associated with building and maintaining a relationship with people. Proper greetings can bring the right association to be the source for relevant guidance, integration, and inclusion in the new learning society. It also indicates how careful, flexible, and respectful one is of other peoples, institutions, and community cultures. Finally, it demonstrates the willingness to identify with the host community in the new learning arena. Moreover, it is a sign of appreciation and desire to be closer to the people in the learning environment.

Misconceptions in Greeting Culture

Previously, I mentioned the effects of cultural misunderstanding. In most cases, greeting from unfamiliar people and cultures may have elements that can confuse the users. So often, people make common mistakes when trying to imitate foreign greeting cultures. For example, most western people shake hands when greeting each other and think shaking hands should go hand in hand with eye contact. Therefore, for such people, these two aspects are significant in their greeting culture that everybody ensures to transmit to their offspring.

So, a similar greeting culture can dominate a large part of the world. For instance, in Europe, Australia, and North America, shaking hands and making eye contact may be typical and appropriate substances of greeting behavior for the majority to observe, at least before the eruption of the coronavirus. At the same time, most western folks believe that if one cannot demonstrate eye contact with someone he greets, there must be something wrong (except where they lean the body forward) with trustworthiness. The funny thing is that such people do not think eye contact conceptualization is not universally applicable, which is the primary reason they get problems understanding other people with different greeting cultures.

Indeed, shaking hands and eye contact has no universal meaning. Besides, some cultures translate shaking hands and even looking at senior people's eyes unwaveringly as a lack of respect. For example, in some societies, people can only perform handshaking and look straight into the eyes of people of their age and those with the same societal positions, but not those who are elderly or senior. Such cultures forbid young people from directly staring at their elders and other important people when greeting. Thus, one must be careful and execute the Greeting thoroughly and correctly without gazing at them continuously. If one fails to perform the salute properly may even face the consequence of their incompetence. The situation is so because they respect such greeting culture, which demonstrates respect differently from most western societies. Therefore, for westerners to comprehend people who originate from such greeting cultures that diverge from them need first to understand the translation of their greeting behavior. Indeed, it may be cynical to generalize or transfer the greeting experience from one society to another.

Variations in Greeting Culture

WE HAVE EXPERIENCED a revolution in greeting cultures due to the coronavirus eruption. The most affected greeting culture is shaking hands and hugging; some groups encourage body contact between the givers and receivers. So, in distancing, people must be creative and accept that even non-handshaking and distance greetings can demonstrate all greeting requirements. For example, there are different greeting cultures; some respect privacy and individual territory by creating distance. The culture of non-handshaking salutation existed even before the coronavirus, especially in non-western societies. People have had this tradition for ages, and it may be an excellent time to turn to such values of distance greeting when we leave behind the handshaking.

In addition, different societies have ways of demonstrating respect and honesty when greeting each other. For instance, in some communities, highly respected people like parents, teachers, religious leaders, and politicians receive distance greetings. The majority welcome these folks differently from how they do to others, and they demonstrate honesty and honor by applying different greeting methods without necessary handshaking. Instead, people take leaders and others with vital roles in their families and societies so seriously that they sometimes bend their knees, look down, or move their bodies forward, as mentioned earlier. In addition, other methods may apply to demonstrate respect rather than eye contact and handshaking, such as removing the male cap or headcover for females.

Sometimes, in some societies, eye contact with respectable people differs from Westerners' point of view. For example, some leaders (society, families, and religion) desire to be contacted with eye contact, allowing the eyes to wander away from them while executing the greeting. For the culture's practitioner, this wandering of the eyes indicates respect and submissiveness, not dishonesty. Someone must look into the eyes for a while, then away, back again, etc. It means one needs not continuously look at the recipients' eyes as most

Westerners would like, and it does not mean anything more than a different greeting culture.

As a student, identify how the previous society's greeting differs from the present. After that, learn the correct way of executing the contextual greeting style from others. There is no equilibrium in greeting between two or more cultures; rather, the act must be perfect without contamination of traditions. Therefore, one should choose a single culture in greeting, preferring a contextual one.

Indeed, the greeting practice is also one of many unwritten rules in different societies which people take for granted. No one has taught a lesson of greeting in humanity or science, maybe in the arts deemed relevant. In the future, I hope the greeting culture may be a topic of interest as higher education stakeholders increase their knowledge about its importance. Undoubtedly, misunderstandings in supervision and advising tasks between students and their learning agencies are often influenced by failure in social relations, starting from greeting. So, knowledge about relational cultures, including greetings, is highly needed in solving the student attrition problem facing most higher education institutions.

Therefore, introducing relational cultures to students' learning packages can save the purpose of students' integration and retention. Furthermore, the more students master the cultural aspects of their learning contexts, the better they become socially motivated to continue with academic tasks. Indeed, as mentioned earlier, the greeting culture is one of the most ignored topics in higher education. Institutional management and curriculum developers assume students have acquired the required greeting habit or can adjust without guidance. Sometimes, they think they should learn informally before admission; hence, no one advises them.

Let us reflect on the issue of "handshaking" or "look away and to the recipient of the greet. The exercise can look and pause, look and pause" without knowing exactly how long one must look at those he greets and how to perform the looking. So, it needs careful observation where students must be willing to learn, receive corrections, and adjust. It is also better to remember that people of the same culture may execute different greetings on different occasions.

Some greetings styles are meant for comforting people in difficult situations, and some greetings demonstrate friendships and excitement. Sometimes, people can hug because they have not seen each other for a long time or comfort each other. However, the majority shake hands during formal greetings, such as in business meetings, interviews, and other formal occasions, while others hug under joyful circumstances. There is no clear distinction between how a greeting should be in formal and informal settings, but the environment and culture control the greeting's appropriateness.

If a student thinks the new greeting style is disturbing and unacceptable to his norms, he must inform the provider. Alternatively, he may demonstrate a sign that may indicate his disagreement. The student may notify the institution and the people responsible for student guidance for advice. Such people can also inform the greeting acceptable in the context. Sharing ideas concerning proper greetings may be fruitful and create knowledge that cannot be obtained otherwise. The student may also ask whether there are cultural aspects he must remember when greeting people than making mistakes. Universities should also ask applicants vital questions concerning greeting culture in the application forms before enrolment to highlight their preferences. Universities should also inform applicants about the cultures expected of them in different arenas to avoid fallacies.

As a student, I want to remind you what my teacher told me; "It is better not to greet people if you cannot perform the act correctly." However, when appropriately mastered and executed, the proper greeting action is the act that may integrate you with people of foreign cultures and can minimize and even eradicate discrimination.

<u>**A simple quiz**</u>

Do you think it is vital discussing greeting culture in higher education? If yes, why?

Chapter 4

The Smiling Tradition

"*I see you*" *smile usually is provided to everybody without the intention of conversing with the receivers. While "I care for you," the smiling style has the opposite characteristics and may consume time.*

Smiling may be a part of greetings in some cultures. Most people think this facial act of smiling goes with greetings, but it is not a universal rule. Some provide a smile without necessarily being accompanied by greetings. To understand whether the smile is a part of the greeting culture, you need to know the smiling elegances of two categories. I call the first smiling style "I SEE YOU," which usually does not accompany greetings. The other kind of smile, "I CARE FOR YOU," tends to accompany the greetings and interest in discovering more about the other person.

Indeed, many societies practice smiles with various meanings, but all fall into the two types mentioned. One may be confused and sometimes create unnecessary misunderstandings without understanding the differences between these two categories. Remember, smiling is a little act of facial expression that allows the muscles to contract around the mouth intentionally," but its impact on people's interactions is enormous. In most cases, people appreciate it when they receive and provide this act of smiling genuinely, especially in a harsh and unfamiliar environment. There are several advantages of a smile that I will discuss later in this book.

But first, I want to discuss the art of smiling because it is one of the most welcoming acts that can attract people to each other. It is one of the essential social tools for integration, and higher education students need to smile at people in their learning environment for acceptance. The correct smile can produce positive results that may be beneficial in interacting with learning agencies and other relevant people. However, in a culture where smiling is not part of greetings, people smile at everybody on different occasions without thought, but at the same time, it does soften the hearts. In a culture where a smile is for everybody, it remains an act of mouth muscle movement without apparent feelings. In contrast, where a smile is part of a greeting and more than "I see you," it expresses the attention and care one has for the other person or people.

The two types of smile actions have some commonalities. They convey some messages whether the smile is provided as a part of greetings or randomly without greeting. Both smiles express the friendly atmosphere, and this friendship is what many students long for in their learning life. It is hard for students to express their gratitude to their supervisors and other learning agencies adequately, but a smile can help. Smiling at each other may be translated as a sign of a friendly atmosphere and appreciation of each other's presence. The smiling environment can support students in many ways, as we will see in a moment.

In most cases, both smiles (I see you and I care for you) transmit the feeling of love from the sender to the recipient(s) and observers. No one can resist the love of a smile, especially when that comes sincerely and free of charge. The smile is a mechanical action no one demands or asks for; it should come automatically without conditionalities. The provider tends to do that for free, and the recipient has nothing to pay than sending the smile back to the sender. The exchange process uniquely brings the participants pleasure, peace, and joy.

Indeed, students, supervisors, and other learning agencies prefer to smile in their contact. As we mentioned, the higher education learning environment has become multicultural in most cases, with participants from different backgrounds. Although most have acquired cultures that may differ from the context norms when they smile, it allows communication between multiple cultures. However, they should similarly use the correct styles and translations to understand each other and communicate when they smile.

During the first meeting, the smiles welcome the recipient (s) and make each person comfortable. In higher education, different events allow people to meet each other, thus, lectures, seminars, or workshops. Some events do not need interaction but listening, receiving information, and observing each other. Others demand discussion and teamwork to solve problems, increase knowledge, and make decisions. As a student, one may observe diverse styles of smiling in such events in the learning environment that can differ from how one is used to. It must not be a scary experience; instead, embrace the act by smiling back and finding its correct translation. Sometimes a smile can create confusion if one is unfamiliar with the style provided, and other times it can be costly to the recipient if one gives a wrong smile.

There are many stories related to smiles that the book cannot contain. I discussed smiling behavior students might need to practice in their current learning institutions compared to their previous societies. The information can benefit all students worldwide, especially international students. Most of these students have had difficulty correctly translating the smile they received from people in their learning environment that oppose their traditions. Some are uncertain about the message accompanied by the smiles they receive; for that reason, they usually provide adverse reactions. A lady, Halima, described.

> *"Where I come from, the smile is part of daily greetings. When people meet, they demonstrate happiness, smile, and even hug each other; they genuinely do it with heart and thoughts. The smile is offered with intention and genuine and is not something to provide when you do not mean that. It is not normal to smile or greet people we do not know or are not our associates. If someone smiles at strangers or gets a smile from a stranger, it must be accompanied by explanations or questions. It might be that the person needs a certain favor or have some questions. It may be about direction (without GPS), shopping, or any other question. Otherwise, it is not normal for people to smile at others without greeting or conversing with them for a minute or more. Likewise, it may cause a misunderstanding if someone smiles randomly or at everybody without apparent reason or interaction. In my culture, people may think the person is not mentally okay, which is considered abnormal behavior. However, smiling to a stranger when you have a question or two or need a favor may motivate the other person to assist".*

Halima's explanation indicated that the smile provided in her previous society was an "I care for you" style. She studied in another community where the smile translated, "I see you." Indeed, it may lead to confusion because she used to provide a smile and ask where the person she smiled at was, but in the new learning community, the style was not applicable. Even though Halima discovered that the smile in the learning environment did not convey the "I care for you" message as in the previous culture, she appreciated receiving and providing it. Indeed, the smile did not cater to the same purpose but demonstrated a friendly and inclusive atmosphere.

Halima continued to describe the new smiling style.

"In this society, I found a trap with the kind of smile provided. People smile widely to anyone, whether they know you or not, but they are not doing it with heart or thoughts. It is just a matter of widening their mouth in both parts and releasing them soon after passing you. The message they desire to send to the recipient is unclear, but at least it makes people comfortable. I am trying to find out what people in this community think the smile is for because they do not have the same meaning as in my previous culture. It was confusing because I was not familiar with this new kind of smile, and often I became uncertain of the response when I got a smile; in the beginning, I had to stop waiting for a question or a word, but people just passed by me and continued with their business without a word.

The surprising thing is that people smile at their fellow humans, animals, and objects; it is getting crazy here; they smile everywhere and at everything. Recently, I asked some friends why they provide such a fake smile when they do not care about me. And what was the purpose of smiling at someone you do not care about? I received different arguments supporting me in realizing that smiling conceptualization in this new community differs from my previous understanding. For the majority, the smile meant nothing more than acknowledging someone's presence by widening and twisting their lips".

Halima is not alone in such confusion concerning smiling. Undoubtedly, students from societies where smiles are part of the greeting and the key to a conversation might have the same challenges Halima described. Any new cultural activities, including the smile, may lead to bewilderment if poorly understood. Halima's explanation indicated that the new learning environment practiced "I *see you*" smiling culture. It is different from "I care for you," and if you have not experienced such kind of smile before, surely you may be confused. Halima said she often stopped waiting for a smile giver's word, but no one provided one. Indeed, "I see you" smile is usually provided to everybody without intending to converse with the receivers. It is easy to execute, and one does not utilize time or change the pace of his movement unless the recipients react otherwise. People broaden their lips while passing by each other; in this case, one can simultaneously be the recipient and receiver of the smile.

Some Supportive Questions

As a student new to the learning society, try to re-examine the smiling style provided around and on different occasions. For example, find out whether the smile is "I care for you" or "I see you," or maybe it combines the two. The combination means that people smile at each other randomly, but when they meet someone they know, they ask about their well-being by conversing a bit. So, ask some questions about what you observe different from the previous experience concerning smiling behavior. The information can help you interact with others appropriately and save time you could waste wandering around full of confusion.

These are some of the questions that can be helpful.

- Do people smile at you randomly, even those you do not know?
- Do you smile back to people who provide a smile to you?
- Are you sensitive and selective about whom to smile at?
- Do people talk to you when they smile at you, or do they just smile and continue their business?

These questions can identify the smile that dominates your learning environment. It is also a good way of learning the differences between the two smiling styles. Although I have informed you of their differences, you may discover several other issues concerning the smile provided in your learning environment. For example, you may realize the smile you experience in the learning environment, or university differs significantly from the surrounding society. Another issue is the benefits of the previous smile habit compared to the current in the new learning institution. So, you may attempt to determine which style you prefer and the reasons for your partialities.

Moreover, surround yourself with people who can help you comprehend the smiling translation. Likewise, train to translate the new smiling act and correctly perform the contextual dominant smiling culture without confusion. Finally, avoid mistakes caused by wrong performance and translation because your failures can chase people away.

The Benefits of Smiling

Everything different from our customs can be hard to accept, tolerate, and practice. It was challenging for Halima and other students to observe the smiling being executed and translated differently from their previous culture. However, Halima and her friends later realized the benefits of the two types of smiles, especially the new "I see you" smile. Although, in the beginning, it was a confusing situation and difficult to cope with, Halima was determined to learn.

In a follow-up conversation, she brought some helpful knowledge about the smiling she doubted. Without her openness, I could not write the benefits of a smile in this book and been able to differentiate between these two styles. Her conversation supports my hypothesis that many students are left behind partly because of the confusion associated with greetings and smiling culture. Now I am writing to you as a reader, a student, or an advisor about these discoveries of smiling I obtained from Halima and other students. The information will help you interact and attract functional and friendly people beyond those you smile at for integration and inclusion in your learning environment.

The Nature of a Smile

As I mentioned, it is vital not to quickly judge whatever new culture you meet in your learning environment. Halima and her fellow students studied to help them understand the smiling culture in the new learning context. I will write some of their findings that may benefit readers of this book. First, they found that the smile provided in their learning environment was unconditional and multiplied. In the beginning, Halima had thought that the new smiling culture created "the smile abusive "behavior, and she thought she would never acquire such "unhealthy practices" of not caring for the other person. She called it a "plastic smile" (that is what she called it before she investigated its benefits).

However, as she continued observing and receiving this kind of smile from people she did not know, she started feeling different and had a happy attitude almost daily. She encountered different circumstances that could be stressful to handle, but what wiped the stress was smiling from others in all the situations. Halima had difficulties with academic tasks and sometimes needed help; she dared to ask for support from people who smiled at her. It could be hard to explain her challenge if people around her were not showing such a smiling attitude.

Indeed, one cannot judge other people's cultures without reflecting on themselves. Halima is a kind of scientist who prefers a quantitative method of investigation. She studied for a master's degree in computer science and is good at mathematics, especially statistics. Therefore, Halima re-examined and compared her previous culture of smiling and the new learning environment. In her independent research about smiling, she realized some benefits and limitations. For example, she discovered that the "I see you" news smiling style had some benefits unavailable in her previous smiling culture.

First, Halima compared the frequency people smiled and the environment that led them to smile. She also investigated to whom the majority provided and received the smile often. The new female student found some practical shortcomings in the smile practices. In her previous smiling culture, smiling was limited to people they knew. Therefore, this affected the frequency they smiled per day, week, and even per year. Sometimes, they could meet a few people they knew daily or weekly, which reduced the frequency they smiled. Even though her community was a multicultural society, they had a similar smiling culture where they smiled only at people they knew. The habit limited smiling because it provided smiles to friends, family members, and other familiar individuals. According to Halima's investigation, she admitted that the habit reduced the occurrence of smiling.

Another discovery Halima came up with was that smiling in her previous culture was associated with cheerful situations. It was like fire burning from the inside and desiring to burn worries and provide peace to the person they smiled at. On the other hand, when people are down to earth with life challenges, they can smile when meeting with someone they know and share their worries for a minute or more. We know that life sometimes brings challenges that may hinder one from being cheerful, and "I care for you smile" is good for those moments in Halima's community.

However, Halima found that even "I see you smile" can bring relief to people who have not met someone they know. She found that a smile was not a priority in her previous culture in many situations and interactions, especially unpleasant ones. For example, one may lose loved ones or encounter family problems, employment challenges, and even accidents without a comforter. Also, sometimes people get sick, and where there are sicknesses or other health challenges in Halima's culture, it is not easy for people to smile.

Typically, the persons in the mentioned challenging situations (sickness, employment, loss of loved ones) had to demonstrate sorrow and discontent. If they smiled, they could create confusion because others could not sympathize with them. The withdrawal of a smile was a sign of calling for sympathy from others in Halima's smiling culture. If the persons with challenges smiled, others could take away their sympathy because they felt they needed no comfort and were strong enough to deal with the challenge. The incidences of unhappiness were inevitable in their everyday lives due to frequent challenging events. So, automatically the situation minimizes the frequency of smiling and even the number of people to smile at. Therefore, the new smiling habit could comfort people regardless of their situation, increasing the smiling atmosphere and frequency.

In Halima's community, People had to smile only when it was genuine, and without that, no smile. For example, one could not just smile and go away without greeting the recipient and demonstrating his concern about the person. However, a genuine smile was not always possible and measured how people extended conversation. The smile and greeting could cost one to five minutes of an individual's time for it to be genuine. Halima discovered that sometimes, people were busy and had no time to ask about others' well-being, which made them avoid smiling and greeting altogether. They thought they had to perform it correctly if they smiled, demonstrating their friendliness and spending some minutes in a conversation. For the smile to be genuine, the senders and recipients had to follow the central protocols, thus, greeting and extended discussion. She concluded that lacking time to provide a genuine smile minimized the smiling frequency.

Another issue that minimizes the smile's frequency, "I care for you," was its restriction to humans. This smile was only for people, not other living organisms like animals and natural objects like flowers. Halima unfolded that they could occasionally stay indoors with cats and dogs or flowers without contact with the outside world. Sometimes, one could be sick or caring for an infant without meeting other people outside their home. They also had several older people who seldom left their homes, and a few came to visit them. Such living conditions minimized contact with people and reduced smile frequency.

Indeed, Halima's evaluation may be generalized to many societies that practice "I care for you" smile style. It means people should learn both styles and evaluate their benefits to their communities. Halima concluded that the previous culture minimized daily smiling frequency and was limited to specific persons. I appreciate her analysis because being able to realize the benefits associated with a foreign culture is a challenging task. Undeniably, some social-cultural acts have several advantages, including greeting and smiling.

Halima apprehended that she received smiles from different people on campus and outside unconditionally in the new culture. Sometimes, she received a smile when she was down and frustrated, and the smiles changed her feelings. Halima was in for the new smile quickly; she even learned to smile at objects and other things apart from humans. The female student smiled almost every day to everyone; the culture seemed pleasant and fit her well. The student objectively reflected on the benefits of the new smiling culture as she did in finding the limits of her previous smile culture.

These are some of the advantages she mentioned. The new smiling culture of the type "I see you" allows people to smile at whomever they come across, even if they do not know each other. This practice creates inclusiveness because smiling at everybody does not cause any misunderstanding of thoughts neither or feelings. Everybody receives and provides a smile, even if it does not include the heart or thoughts about the person, but brings the required inclusion atmosphere.

Second, she discovered that "I see you" smile reduces tension between people who may have met for the first time. Sometimes, meeting with someone for the first time in the learning environment may need preparation. However, if you smile at people, the action may release tension when meeting a stranger. In addition, the act can be an excellent opener to the conversation and create more attention, friendship, and integration. Even if new people have nothing to discuss, smiling at each other may make them want to discuss something, and the conversation may be more pleasant. Sometimes, you may find people automatically smiling at each other and talking about environmental change, God, or war somewhere in the world.

Moreover, the smile, "I see you," can change moods from bad to good; it may change attitudes from depression or isolation to happiness and inclusion. The power of this type of smile is vivid in many situations. Sometimes, a smile may save the purpose when people demonstrate disagreement or agreement. For example, I will explain an episode between a woman, Selina, and a shopkeeper. The woman, Selina, was furious with the shopkeeper because he short-changed her. The woman came to buy some items, paid and left the shop without counting the money she had received from the shopkeeper. On her way home, some meters away after purchasing the food items, she counted the charges and realized that the shopkeeper had short-changed her. So, she realized that the amount she received back from the shopkeeper was not the correct amount she deserved.

Normally, Selina was supposed to count the money before leaving the shop, but she did not check. When she discovered the problem, she was distressed and returned to the shopkeeper to explain her situation. The shopkeeper disagreed with her and acknowledged paying her the correct amount. She tried a smiling technique and talked politely with the shopkeeper explaining how trustworthy the shopkeeper had been to her and the family for a long time. Selina mentioned that her confidence in the shopkeeper led her not to care about counting the money on the spot. While smiling, she mentioned the rules of counting the money before leaving the shop and admitted her fault for not doing so. Therefore, she blamed herself and admitted to learning from the mistake while smiling.

When the shopkeeper saw her smile, and Selina was not blaming him but herself, he became willing to pay the difference. He smiled back, saying, *"Yes, you are among my best customers who have made this shop exist. The issue of short charge has never happened before, so I cannot see why your claim should be false today".* After the statement, where both were smiling, the shopkeeper handed Selina the rest of the money. The woman was excited and thankful for his understanding, and the case favored her based on a smile.

The story justifies how important a smile can be in a misunderstanding situation. It can change the mood and create a willingness to cooperate in some circumstances. If the woman did not smile and become polite, the issue could not be in her favor, and the shopkeeper was legitimately right to refuse the money. The incidence aligns with what Halima perceived as the ability of a genuine smile. She discovered that a smile could change people's minds from negative to positive and even alter the perception of someone who is " cruel" to be "a friend."

Most people tend to be friendlier if they obtain a smile than when they do not receive or provide one. Halima realized that a smile brings a positive feeling to people, even if they do not talk to each other. The friendly and welcoming feeling can engulf people who receive and provide a smile. These feelings may open for discussion and can be the key to the most functional and continuing interaction.

Starting a conversation with a stranger with no smiling face may be challenging. The seriousness of an individual's face can bring fear and uncertainty about whether the discussion will be successful. Sometimes, people can postpone meeting someone simply because the person seems serious without a smiling face. Interacting with persons who lack smiling faces can often be challenging, and the dialogue may not be as friendly as the one accompanied by a smile. As I mentioned, meeting with an outsider may be accompanied by tension and strange feelings if the people involved do not demonstrate a smiling attitude. The moment the persons smile at each other such feelings of anxiety can melt immediately. Most HE students undertake their studies in a new learning environment where they meet strangers, even if when it is in their country. Therefore, creating a smiling and friendly face can invite people and open them for discussion and integration.

According to "I see you smile," the actors can smile at objects just like humans. The practice sounded strange to Halima initially, but she found some advantages to doing that. She discovered that this smile style pays attention to everything surrounding, increasing the smiling regularities per day or week. When people smile at animals and objects, they see them and know the danger or benefits associated with the object or animals involved. This kind of smile increases attention to an individual's surroundings because people meet with different objects and animals almost daily, and some may be dangerous or need help.

Providing a smile at such things demonstrates that one has acknowledged their presence. At the same time, it increases smiling frequencies which may also increase the feeling of joy and calmness in the smile giver. Randomly smiling is often observed when people from "I see you smile" visit gardens, national parks, or natural environments. They normally smile at things they observe as if they are dealing with humans. This act of appreciation through smiling was vivid to Halima, and she found it helpful to some people. She realized that smiling at animals and nature, such as flowers, scriptures, mountains, and others, acknowledges the beauty of the creator's work.

The other important issue about the new smiling style, Halima and her team discovered, is that the new smile is contagious, and if someone provides one smile, he may get back more than one depending on the nature (If the smile was to an object, no smile back). The number of people observed, received, and responded to the smile. Halima concluded that the smile, "I see you," has high reoccurrences than "I care for you." This conclusion supported her and others in changing and learning the new contextual smiling style and performing it appropriately. Halima has acquired both types of smile traditions, and she executes them interchangeably based on the appropriate situation.

Halima's judgment concerning the reoccurrence and the benefit of a smile is essential in higher education learning. Indeed, a smile is one of the magical acts that can benefit someone cognitively, physiologically, and socially. Halima informed me that she was concerned with this act of facial expression and had obtained useful knowledge. She even read scholarly documents to determine whether scientists have something to say about smiling.

The female student, Halima, contended that most scholars believe smiling changes body fluids from furious to calm. In addition, scholars indicate that a smile can release stress and pain from the people involved and increase the individual's immune system. Certainly, people who smile often tend to reduce the tension that could cause high blood pressure and other diseases. So, smiling is one of the simple therapeutic acts that can reduce the risk of diverse health problems. Therefore, with the discussed information in mind, students in higher education should be encouraged to practice smile acts acceptable in their context and learn the translation. As a result, a smile may eradicate isolation and open different opportunities in one's learning environment.

Chapter 5

The Magic of a Smile

Indeed, the act of smiling has many memories. In the previous chapter, a female student, Halima, investigated a smile she found in a new learning environment. Her investigation showed that both "I see you" and "I care for you" smiles are vital for creating a friendly atmosphere. The female student's investigation reminded me of my days when I was a teacher. I taught high school students in chemistry class one day, and smiling helped me immensely. I conducted experiments with students while the nearby class students shouted and argued about something. I did not understand their problem, but I could not communicate with my students in such a noisy environment. Finally, I had to do something to let the students in the other class be quiet and keep order.

Nevertheless, I did not know what to say because they were the most stubborn science students. I was a young and newly employed teacher without much experience with high school nutty boys. I had heard from other teachers that the students felt pleasure in harassing people and had no regard for teachers. I desired to release my students and call it a day, but the examinations were around the corner; they had to perform some experiments. I could not know what to do or how to handle the case in favor of the chemistry students.

Indeed, a smile can help even where there is chaos. As a new female and young teacher, dealing with stubborn high school students may be unpleasant, which is not what most teachers desire. I was scared to approach such character boys, but I had a conducive learning environment for my students. I was disturbed, and my worries were combined with anger and frustration because the noise was unbearable. The students in my class looked at me and said, "Can you tell the students in the neighbor class to stop shouting, Madam? They did not understand the inner conversation and terrible feelings that were going on inside my mind. The nearby class students were increasing their arguments, and it seemed like they were about to fight. Everything was in unusual noise and chaos, and my anxiety increased. The more they shouted and demonstrated disagreement in their class, the more they raised their voices and increased confusion. I could not continue teaching because the students could hardly hear what I was instructing them.

Therefore, I was about to report the incident to the department's head, but I thought it could sound immature and silly. So, I decided to move into the chaotic classroom to discover the problem. I prepared for fight or flight and tried to find the appropriate words for the stubborn students. On the one hand, I thought of frightening them with punishment such as suspension or writing letters to their parents/guardians. But on the other hand, I was also thinking of a friendly conversation where I would ask them politely to stop the commotion. Sincerity, I was unclear on what to communicate with the students, but I entered the classroom anyway.

Contrarily, when I stepped in, I found myself smiling because they were scattered all over the room while pointing fingers at each other. Instead of asking students what was happening and blaming them for creating such a noisy atmosphere, I kept smiling at them while looking at them. Almost all the students who noticed my smile became silent, and some smiled back. The atmosphere changed, and even those unaware of the smile knew something had happened and noticed the quietness. So, they stopped and paid attention to what had occurred; then, they looked at me. I just extended a genuine smile until almost all the students smiled back. Then, I said to them, "thank you very much for the silence because I will be able to teach the nearby chemistry class. I continued that we have examinations in the coming weeks, and today's practice is essential for the students. So, your silence means a lot for them and me; thank you very much".

A smile can do what words cannot. All the students agreed with me to be silent at that very moment. However, most replied with nutty words such as welcome sweety, madam, welcome baby, etc. I did not confront them for their wording that was not appropriate to the setting. I did not even say anything more because the smile fixed everything. The chaotic atmosphere vanished, and they became silent. I returned to the laboratory, and they kept the quiet atmosphere I requested. My chemistry students and I managed to learn until the end of the lesson without hearing from the nutty boys.

Although they called me names, they should not have. I did not mind because that was not my objective. The goal was a silent atmosphere, so I did not follow the other mentioned issues of calling me names. Indeed, the whole process can tell the power of smiling, and my words did not convince them to be silent. Instead, the smile I provided them made the right thing in their mind, and they complied with my request. So, if one smile can be so powerful even to silence the chaos, it is worth practicing how to smile correctly. Indeed, a smile may create a magic result if executed perfectly and with good intentions. Therefore, it is worth learning the art of smiling in the learning environment and executing it in the right way, at the right time, and for everyone.

The smiling action is significant and may even stop suicide and solve social and psychological problems. For example, I heard of this man who wanted to commit suicide by jumping from a bridge, but one policeman saw him and smiled at him when he was about to jump. When the man saw the smile from the policeman, he paid attention and asked why he was smiling. He had never seen a policeman smiling at him but accusing him of doing something wrong. So that day and moment were not ordinary to the man; that is the main reason for him to ask the policeman why he was smiling. The policeman immediately said, "I am smiling because I have good news for you, which I want to tell you before you jump and vanish." The man curiously asked what that was. The policeman continued smiling, and without knowing what the man lacked in his life, he said, "I have a job for you." Then the man smiled at him and said, "I hope you are not kidding me," the policeman said, "not at all, follow me." So, the man stopped his suicide mission and followed the policeman. No one knows what happened next, but the policeman's smile stopped the man from committing suicide.

Therefore, as a higher-education student, do not hesitate to learn the style and translation of the smiling habit that dominates your learning environment. The major issues students should consider in learning about a smiling culture are observing, evaluating, learning, and practicing appropriately. Finally, one day one may wonder about being able to solve personal, social, and integration problems through smiling behavior.

Indeed, smiling in the learning environment may hinder many students from dropping out of their studies. Therefore, one should consider smiling in group discussions, seminars, workshops, and other events. Nothing is more confusing than working with people who are not friendly, so demonstrate your friendly attitude by smiling at others and receiving them appropriately.

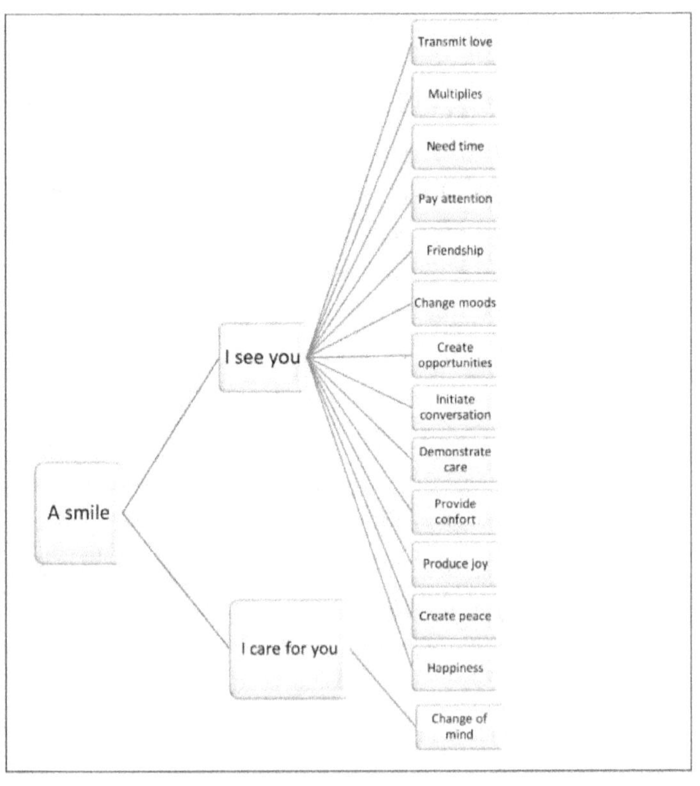

Figure 4. The Multiple Benefits of a Smile

Figure four consists of the various advantages of a smile. Based on my explanation of the smile and the nature of the two styles, "I see you" and "I care for you," the figure provides the function a smile can perform. Please sort out these functions and group them into where they fit most between the two styles. Then, you can rank the benefits based on what a smile can do in your culture. Remember, one benefit can appear in both types, so repeating and indicating the benefits in both smiling styles is acceptable. Therefore, fill the table. Good luck!

Table1. The advantage of smile; "I see you" and "I care for you"

I see you	I care for you
E.g., Inclusive	Selective

Challenges Associated with Smiling

Although smiling has different benefits, it can also bring challenges to practitioners. Halima's experience, the policeman, and mine can motivate you to learn to smile often and correctly. The smile, "I see you," can release the tension you might have encountered in your learning environment, so do not wait for the smile, "I care for you." Although the smile "I see you" is supposed to end soon after passing by someone, you may extend if you are a beginner. Please give it a trial and let it be a part of the training staff and daily practice to master it. Yes, initially, it may be difficult to stop smiling immediately after passing by someone if you come from the "I care for you" smile community. Other times when you practice "I see you" smile, the action may lead to showing your teeth or even making a little laughter sound. Those are little mistakes to avoid, but do not be discouraged; keep on practicing.

I must caution you that laughing in response to "I see you smile" may create a severe misunderstanding. It may be confusing because the smile giver may think you ridicule his smile. I also understand the difficulties of finding a limit and balance between these two smiling styles. Similarly, smiling and laughing or making small agreements sounds like Mhh,

Ohio, needs some care. People unfamiliar with "I see you" smile now and then when you smile at them; they laugh and even make some sound that confuses those who execute the smile. If you are performing "I see you," smile; the principle is silence, so do not make any sound or laugh. Similarly, do not mind hearing such a sound from the recipient(s); it indicates that the person is unfamiliar with the style. Therefore, as a learner, ensure you understand and perform the smile technique correctly to avoid unnecessary misinterpretation.

Although it may be hard for some people to smile, "I see you" style by just moving their lips without involving the heart, I am sure they can obtain perfection in their actions if they keep practicing and perfecting their smile actions and reactions. According to Halima's investigation, learning the "I see you" style is vital, and mastering it is like winning a gold bar due to its multiple benefits, refer to figure four. Besides, smiling is the second social-cultural essential for students to succeed in their learning by attracting people; it is a savior of any isolation situation.

Every postsecondary institution's student must learn, regardless of discipline, learning environment, or background. Scholarly literature has informed the isolation students experience in higher education, often leading to dropout. So, encouraging students to practice smiling actions and reactions to each other can minimize the problem. Besides, every person in diverse societies and cultures smiles, including poor, rich, sick, and healthy they sometimes smile.

Even if smile activities decrease with age or life experiences, some people smile whenever they can. Thus, I am not introducing a new culture by writing about smiling but emphasizing its importance in the learning environment for integration and fighting isolation. So it might be as a reader, and you did not know how important it is before now, so spread the information. Therefore, learning to smile appropriately and translate the smile correctly in a new learning environment should no longer be a problem.

So, keep smiling.

A Word of Caution

Smiling may leave a memory on the practitioners' faces, especially if one smiles often. Some people are sensitive about their facial expressions and wrinkles, particularly women (sorry to say this). So, adjusting yourself and correctly smiling can help avoid unnecessary smiling wrinkles. If you carefully pay attention to your facial expression, smiling will not change your face negatively. But, if you are careless, it can cost your facial appearance by causing wrinkles, particularly for those who already have smile dimples.

In most cases, one can avoid such unnecessary wrinkles by practicing smiling correctly. The first step is to ensure you relax the muscles around your mouth when the smile is unnecessary. You may even practice before a mirror to see the most affected area on your face when smiling to focus on it. Second, you may have regular massage to the site you notice affected by applying some moisturizer lotion that delays wrinkles. Thirdly, avoid exposing your face to the sun without applying sun lotion because that may dry your skin and allow wrinkles to develop when smiling.

However, by any means, the challenge of wrinkles development should not hinder anyone from smiling. On the contrary, enjoying the provision and reception of smiling should be part of one's daily routine. The process may bring some fortune one has never seen before. Even if the practitioners have some wrinkles on their faces and do not have time to treat them, as I proposed, most people have no difficulties understanding the situation. Developing smiling wrinkles is often a compliment because it indicates that one smiles. So, as a student, smile without fear.

This information about smiling is essential, although academics may consider it irrelevant and a waste of their precious time. The opposers of such soft and social messages may think HE learning is only for hard scientific learning materials, not how to smile. It is good to believe that postsecondary students should learn the academic stuff related issues, but they cannot avoid meeting people. Most higher education folks desire to work with academic disciplinary issues neglecting the social aspects of becoming better citizens and skilled laborers. A lack of social knowledge and how to get well with people by applying smile principles has caused disaster in most universities. Students should share their knowledge with others and know key openers of vital conversations.

Unfortunately, university management and other officials dealing with students may not see the significance of learning to greet and smile at people. Simultaneously, the same people can complain when students do not demonstrate the expectations of social characters in different circumstances. I am here to say that small issues, actions, and reactions academics ignore lead to student attrition. So, let us start with the smallest issues before solving algebra or formulating academic theories.

Ultimately, I want to emphasize that greetings and smiling are essential issues in the postsecondary learning environment. Take it from me; the insight of appropriate greeting cultures, including smiles, can bring you treasures that philosophy and mathematics may not. Failure to perform mathematics equations correctly can have fewer disadvantages than failure to greet and smile at people accordingly. So, keep smiling ☺ ☺ ☺.

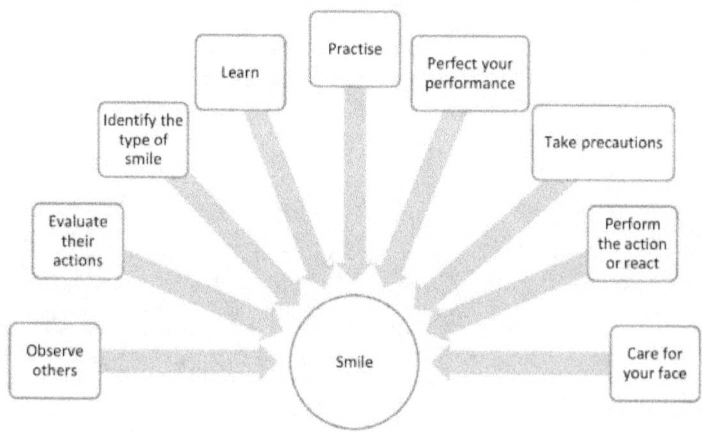

Figure 5. The Process to Perfect Smiling

Figure five demonstrates nine essential stages of perfecting your smile correctly. When smiling, the first thing to do is observe others in your learning environment and the community. Moreover, evaluate their smiling actions and reactions to each other to identify their type. Understand which type dominates in the context and learn how to practice while receiving feedback on the performance. Furthermore, it would help if you continue practicing and perfecting the smiling act to avoid confusion while caring for facial appearance. Thus, one may observe these steps to master the process and succeed in being part of the learning community regardless of location and learning demands. Indeed, mastering social-relational aspects of greetings and smiling can allow one to study anywhere in the globe without facing isolation.

Chapter 6

Dress Code Culture

Academics and students think they can wear anything, and nobody cares about their appearance. Thinking less about the dress code is a misconception that students should not possess if they desire to succeed in postsecondary education.

The dress code in postsecondary learning environments differs from other formal education levels. Most high schools in different countries encourage students to wear uniforms and identify with the institution's dressing norms. Therefore, first-year university students from high school with uniform philosophy may have challenges finding the appropriate dress to wear in liberal higher education institutions. It means students from institutions bond with uniforms may cross-dress code boundaries without guidance concerning dressing culture. According to the informants, most have had problems choosing what to wear on different occasions. Universities neglect to inform their students of the desired dress code; in some cases, they assume students may discover themselves creating challenges.

In some cases, academics and students think they can wear anything, and nobody cares about their appearance. I do not mean one should not wear what he is used to or the dress from his culture or origin but should marry the occasion. Thinking less about the dress code is a misconception that university students should not possess if they desire to succeed. Professional individuals' appearance matters more than how some students think about it. People may say they do not mind what you wear or how you appear and the outfit, but do not always believe them; instead, they look proficient. The people who speak lightly about dress codes are the first to condemn when students break contextual dress norms.

Simultaneously, information from social media where some people preach independence in dressing and personal freedom in appearance should not stop students from wearing according to the institution's cultural norms. Often some encourage people to wear whatever they like and appear to be the same people wearing appropriately. Still, they can also be the same people who judge others by their outfits and may leave those whose clothes are not pleasing aside and pick others in case of professional opportunities. The problem is when a student does not look the way expected for the occasion, especially in official meetings and gatherings. As a student, if you have not started being observant of the dress code in the learning environment, start today. Find out the appropriate dress code the majority put on different occasions.

All in all, dressing smartly as a university student is vital. Regardless of what others think of you, it is better to be smart and stylish than shabby and hopeless. I am not talking about excessive and expensive dressing, but professional based on the contextual desired culture. The smartness you demonstrate from the outside may force you to create the same look from the inside, mentally and emotionally. In addition, the bright physical appearance and academic capability may bring you some unexpected opportunities. So, learn to have some values in dressing even when you are uncomfortable, disappointed, and busy preparing for learning and examinations. Do not undermine your dressing simply because you will sit in the library or lecture room. It does not mean being fashionable and dynamic with up-to-date expensive outfits, but you may create two or more garments that make you look presentable, acceptable, and academically.

Students in higher education need to demonstrate that learning is not a punishment where there is no time to soap up and look good. Therefore, students should appear fresh, happy, and professionally ready for whatever occasion in their learning environment. Learning in postsecondary institutions is not for making individuals shabby and unworthy but for molding them socially, academically, and privately as professionals. Therefore, students must dress according to the occasion (seminar, workshop, group discussion, lecturers) without apologizing for being professional and smartly dressed.

As a student, you are in a learning environment where professionals probably work with diverse people of different backgrounds. People with various dressing cultures should have freedom of dressing because having a uniform for all can deprive them of their right to be themselves. Even though the learning cooperation can be physical or online, individually or in groups, an appropriate appearance may increase partners' collaboration. Students might be in a multicultural learning environment where people wear different dresses without restrictions but should care for the acceptable contextual ones.

Indeed, wearing smart and attractive can boost students' confidence in contacting others, hence integration and inclusion. Most HE learning environments are mixtures of many settings, such as family scenes, teaching and learning arenas, and socializing. Other sites in higher education can be a friend-finding center, a spouse-seeking context, and a background-checking post. Therefore, the list can go on and on about what higher education learning institutions can be for some people. So, the higher education learning context may be students' present, future, and everything. It is the most complex learning environment that cannot be defined but can only be theorized, labeled, and experienced as an "academic environment" for its highest good of knowledge and skills. Even though it is a juggle of diverse individuals with various needs and expectations, it is a learning environment because everyone should learn something. Therefore, higher institutions' learning environments are the most sensitive setting that provides unique experiences to participants.

One of the types of knowledge students should observe appropriately is social relational issues. Indeed, recognizing appropriate cloth for such a complex environment can be demanding but worth students' time. First, understanding the dress required may support them to be respectable members of the academic community and beyond. If you are uncertain about the professional dress code, consult others, including your advisors and supervisors.

I assume every institution has a professional dress they prefer and consider typical even if they do not advise. One needs to take a break and look around to find the dressing culture in the learning environment. Students must investigate how people appear in seminars and workshops on campus and outside. Likewise, students find dressing style change according to the events and differently in lectures, laboratories, and other gatherings.

Undoubtedly, students willing to learn may discover contextual dress codes quickly. Finding the appropriate outfits is essential whether you are learning online or physically. Indeed, you must observe what to wear when communicating with your peers and other learning agencies. No one expects you to appear shabby or wear unacceptable clothes online or in physical settings.

For example, online learning is not professional to wear a night dress or swimming garments if such clothing does not save the purpose. It might bring an ill translation if you are not dealing with a swimming lesson or drama. If you wear such a dress outside their context, you demonstrate your unawareness of professional clothing. No one will punish students for wearing unprofessional, but some opportunities may pass by, and such an experience can be a kind of unspoken reprimand.

Professional Dressing

Professional dress depends on the institution's code of conduct and society's dressing culture. For example, people have different professional clothing styles in each continent, country, and community. Higher education professional dressing can be anything from suits and miniskirts most Westerners identify themselves with to kanga and kitenge of African and Indian or Japanese costumes. I suppose every institution and community has a dress code the majority prefer to utilize and regard as appropriate in their learning environments.

In most cases, it is not customary for university students to appear in uniforms unless the institution is out of the ordinary. Indeed, special institutions may have the dress code known to their participants in advance. However, most university students can choose what to wear daily and on different occasions. In addition, the institution and society's dress preferences tend to change with events and resources. So, students must also observe academic and non-academic dress codes to fit in the new learning environment. Individual observation, evaluation, and learning are essential qualities to merge into the learning environment dress code.

Considering the dress code may be the most critical culture to observe when you arrive at the university if you desire to be part of the learning community. One student, Alice, informed me about her experience in HE abroad when we discussed dressing culture. She asserted.

"I remember when I studied for a master's degree abroad, there were times I did not know what to wear because almost all my dresses differed from many other students. I was a banker before admission to a master's degree in accounting. I had no other dress that suited the learning environment except suits and party dresses. At the university, I continued wearing suits as usual because that was my professional and daily style. Besides, I had no other types of clothes apart from ceremonial ones because I did not need them. At the university, my fellow students often asked me if I would go somewhere else after lectures or if I had a seminar or workshop outside the university campus. I became tired of such questions almost every day; I realized later that my dress was the reason behind all the questions. So, I started examining my dress compared to my peers and other learning agencies, including advisors and supervisors. I found that I was wearing clothes that, for most people in the context, indicated special occasions or special events. The University dress code differed from my daily dress, so they translated it that way.

Indeed, for the institution and society, wearing suits indicated an idea of a special occasion or a state of being in a high class. Due to such translations, most academics did not desire to position themselves higher than the rest of the community members, so they dropped off wearing suits on normal days. So, when I dressed in a suit on regular bases, their translation was like I was informing them that "I am of high class." According to the institution's dress code, such were the messages I conveyed to them through my clothing.

Nothing disturbing to a stranger like ignorance of social-cultural norms. I gradually realized that most of my fellow students and academics wore jeans and t-shirts or shirts in regular classes. They wore suits during conferences or seminars, mostly when the presenters or some audiences were from abroad. Some lecturers had wardrobes in their offices to change whenever the situation changed in their teaching schedule. For instance, a teacher could wear jeans and a t-shirt, let us say, in the morning lecturers. If, after the lectures, there was a seminar with a foreign presenter, he could change his outfit to a suit, mini skirt, or any other clothes they thought relevant for the event. Depending on the circumstances, this clothes shifting could happen even more than once a day. Otherwise, people were wearing casual and different from my dressing style".

The explanation by Alice indicates the typical situation that exists in some HEIs with dress codes. Luckily, the female student was observant and investigative of other people's outfits and managed to compare and judge her clothing accordingly. In addition, her awareness of differences in dress codes between her previous work environment and the current learning context encouraged her to be inquisitive and adjust to the appropriate dressing quickly.

Sometimes, the dress code is not something to be taught, but finding out information and observing may help students understand the dressing practice required. Just as Alice watched and learned what was wrong with her dressing, based on the questions he received, one may soon realize what he should wear without being told. The basic principle is to desire to be part of the learning community through the outfit's appearance. Alice realized the institution had a dress code, which she did not observe from the beginning, so she received some unexpected questions which brought awareness.

Indeed, students must not wait to be questioned or left alone for them to consider wearing the appropriate dress code seriously. Waiting for someone to alert them can be late because not everyone prefers asking questions or informing others of their weaknesses. Most people think that informing others what to do without their consent can bring an insult. Thus, everyone ought to be observant and make an appropriate judgment on dressing habits without creating a possibility of discrimination or isolation. The students' observation and correct decision in their dressing must be a priority and purposive project to undertake. It is not all right to see students isolated or discriminated against because of their outfits.

Dressing Controversies

Institutions' management must consider that a lack of information concerning the dress code is challenging for students. The institutions seldom write to the applicants informing them in advance of the type of clothes. Although it is vital information one could receive, the institutions ignore providing such guidance to their applicants. I have gone through different university web pages, reading the information they provide to their applicants, but the dress code is absent. We do not read from the admission requirements about the institution's outfits; you can also quickly check universities' web pages as a reader. Most students learn about dressing after enrolment and sometimes regret joining the institution. The dressing information should be part of the social-cultural aspects, and students should acquire information before enrolment for their preparation.

Enrolling in higher education institutions can be challenging, especially where dress styling differs from students' preferred style. Some students lack the dress required to amalgamate in the learning environment. For example, Alice had no other clothes to wear than those she used as a banker. In the extended conversation, she informed me that she had to buy new clothes to fit into the learning environment. Lack of dressing knowledge in advance disturbed her financially for the whole semester, and if she had no such resources to purchase new dresses, she could feel uncomfortable for a long time. The disturbing situation in Alice's study life was due to the university's lack of information concerning appropriate outfits. The information could benefit her most before enrolment and save her financially.

The dress code is one of the ignored issues by many universities. I think universities should inform students about clothing in their application forms. Furthermore, I think universities should propose the dress code preferred for different occasions such as parties, conferences, and seminars (to mention a few). Appearance is one of the essential aspects of integration, which can open or close some doors for students. Even for the institutions that people think do not regard dressing culture seriously, these institutions have dress codes only that no one verbalizes to students or academics.

When I thought of information students must acquire concerning HE's dress code, I discussed the topic with one academic master, David, at one University. Here is what he advised.

"In our university, students can wear whatever they like without being instructed. However, clothing usually informs a lot about the person and can attract or repel some people. Although clothes are for body protection, they also convey information about the person wearing them, including his thinking and feelings. For example, when we blend with other people from different cultures, we convey our friendly and inclusive perception through our outfits. The behavior can bring acceptance and cooperation

that could not exist. Wearing cloth from another culture indicates your wishes for acceptance and willingness to be vulnerable to their culture. The cloth informs people of the other culture that you are ready and flexible in your perception and actions concerning the current cultural values. You do not regard the previous culture as the only best culture in the world, but you also admire and accept other cultures, including those you wear the garments of".

David, the academic master, and psychologist, added, *"Clothes may also convey information about the person and what he stands for. For instance, when we wear the uniform of the organization or company we work for, we share the identity of being part of the company and its ideology. We are also obliged to display the conduct acceptable by the company; we dress in its uniform because we represent the company. When we stand out from a group by wearing different outfits from the rest of the group members, we convey some information that may indicate self-appreciation, pride, and even the power of our individuality or culture. On the other hand, it may inform the lack of resources to purchase what others possess. We may even demonstrate the difficulties we encounter in merging into the group and our desire or undesired to do so.*

Therefore, although the institution does not dictate what one should wear, the proper dress code in our community is the one that makes someone comfortable, approachable, and acceptable. So, suppose a student desires to be part of the learning community. In that case, he has to demonstrate his desire verbally and through his appearance, including dressing, to say," Yes, we do not have a unique dress in this University, but we have a dress code. As a result, most students gradually learn to be part of our community after enrolment."

Although David indicated the lack of a uniform or dress style, you can learn from his explanation that a dress code is desired and required of students. He also described that the information about the dress code is not provided to students in advance. However, students' realization of the institutional dress style tends to be clear after enrolment. He did not mention this dress code for the institution, but he was smart-looking and dressed when we had the conversation. Also, most of the teachers and students at the University were professionally smart-looking. Therefore, it is up to the individual student to learn to observe the dress code to be part of the learning institution and the community or ignore it, facing isolation. David's description indicated that students are the ones to compromise with the institution and society's dress code for their successful integration.

David communicated similar information as Alice described her situation, only that his explanation verbalized the concern differently. Alice had to learn the dress code appropriately after embarrassment and differentiated the dress required on different occasions. This kind of learning is what Mr. David informed when he mentioned: "Students learn gradually the dress required of them." Therefore, as a student who desires to understand what to wear, you must be observant of others. If you are part of the learning community and desire to merge, try to imitate social-cultural aspects, including dressing. Personal observation is applicable when there are no written rules and uniformity. Therefore, higher education students must observe, learn, and imitate the contextual dress code.

Special Dress Code

Consequently, special institutions tend to have dressing uniformity. Some are private institutions, and others are governmental and outstanding organizations. Some have dress rules that differ from students' previous institutions or workplaces. These universities tend to have specific dress codes that all students and, in some cases, academics must observe. For example, most military and religious-owned institutions normally have uniformity in the dress. They also inform the applicants of their preferences, and such preliminary information about the dress code is vital for students.

In addition, the information about clothing provided by such institutions supports students in deciding whether to join the institutions. Such institutions normally have extraordinary learning beliefs and systems out of the ordinary. Thus, failure to dress according to the institution's recommended uniform may jeopardize an individual's membership and learning opportunities. For example, one student, Stella, informed that her university, owned by a religious organization, prohibits wearing trousers for female students on the University campus. Students can wear such a dress outside the campus and will not face any problems, but if they attempt to dress within the campus, they may face suspension and lose their admission.

Furthermore, Stella said female students could not associate with male students in lectures, seminars, or workshops. They should position themselves separately during these events, primarily on the university's campus. Suppose female students mix with male students for inevitable learning reasons, such as working in the laboratories and doing some group assignments. In that case, the female must change her dress and cover her head. Clothing by covering the head is among the dress code for female students in this religious institution.

Similarly, in most institutions, the student's graduation has special garments. We usually witness diverse graduation dress types in different colors and designs students wear in casual dresses. The official clothes minimize the stress related to casual dresses for graduation. After the official graduation party, students with no private parties tend to stay in their dresses under special garments. However, those who desire to hold private ceremonies must cover the cost of another dressing if they prefer to appear different from the uniform. It may seem to double the price; first, the official party's expense with the University where they must hire or buy the graduation garments. Second, the costs for their private party dress where students celebrate their victory with family and friends. Recognizing the dress code required for every occasion in the learning environment may benefit students to budget appropriately and amalgamate in diverse situations.

On the other hand, standing unique in dressing style is a quality one must proudly demonstrate where acceptable. Do not shy to be different from others in the learning environment if you feel more comfortable, integrated, and functional. It might be part of advertising your cultural distinctiveness by not dressing like anybody else in the learning community. Yes, a student with some reasons may decide to stand out from the department, institution, and community dress code without being prohibited. However, it may raise some critics, questions, and unfamiliar comments. So, prepare for it and find strategies to handle the situation of being unique and its consequences without ill feelings. We can now understand that lacking information on the importance of proper dressing and other outfit issues may hinder students' integration and cause isolation.

Appropriate Dressing

As discussed, a proper dress code depends on the institution, event, and resources. It does not mean when you wear clothes resembling everybody else, and you fulfill the requirement of appropriate dress. It does not mean dressing is the only criterion for integration, but it is an element of many factors that can facilitate students' integration. Sometimes, when students observe and practice the existing dress code, as David said, they demonstrate their willingness to be part of the new community's social culture. It creates a lively connection with others because the dress speaks about the owner louder than the words. So, dress according to the context acceptability and be presentable in your learning environment to save the purpose. It may be one tool that promotes students' cooperation and motivation to associate with others in the new society.

Suppose you are appointed to represent your class at a conference or certain academic or social events; people desire to see you presentable. Sometimes, the selection happens partly because of your dress code, observant behavior, and other intellectual and social qualifications. Sometimes, different favors may come your way by merely dressing correctly; it may be accompanying your supervisor in educational meetings, leading social events, or delivering a speech about something in the field. Although academic qualifications such as appropriate knowledge and skills of the issue are vital, dress habits can separate you from others with the same educational qualifications.

It is human nature to be attracted to beauty. Therefore, being smartly dressed is not a regretful idea in the postsecondary learning environment. People can be eager to listen to your presentation simply because you dress accordingly. However, it does not mean that dressing is the only essential social quality students should focus on; it indicates the seriousness and cares for the event. I am not telling you to unnecessarily use your study time to make your physical appearance attractive; NO, not, because appearance alone may not take you far. Every student should combine appearance with other social and academic qualities required to succeed. In my books concerning higher education, I have informed different qualities students should acquire to succeed.

Thus, as a higher-education student, I do not think you desire to open to unnecessary outfit critics by wearing anyhow. Dress informs several issues when you stand before other people. First, before you present anything to the audience, you must re-evaluate your appearance. Most of the time, when a presenter appears to the audience, the first thing which attracts the audience is his appearance. Some universities, especially those that mind students and academic dress and appearance, tend to place mirrors in each corridor for the stakeholders to check themselves. These mirrors are not for decoration but for everyone in the institution to care for their appearance. Observing such facilities in your institution signifies that the management cares for the dress code and desires its members to look professional.

Again, beauty attracts, and the opposite is repeal. It is usual for some folks to distance themselves from less attractive things, including human beings. The behavior of selectivity may be unfortunate to some people, but it happens all the time because that is what it is. Yes, it is like that; we normally attract to beauty sometimes unconsciously. However, things or people can be beautiful but misplaced, and unnecessary items or factors may cover their beauty. The disclosure applies to students who dress inappropriately, which may cloud their professional appearance.

For example, the majority do not dress according to the events; refer to the changing of cloth I mentioned earlier for some academics within the institution. It shows that wearing is appropriate according to the circumstances and context; otherwise, it will be a kind of displacement appearance that can also reduce beauty. When students dress appropriately, the observers desire to learn more about their academic progress. As a student, discovering more about your appearance and paying attention to dress details may lead to people requiring your knowledge and skills. However, it would be best to avoid misplacement caused by wearing outfits contrary to the event, such as party dress in academic meetings, and vice versa.

Ultimately, it all depends on the individual student's cultural sensitivity decision. Everyone must consider the dressing consequences without being forced or creating ill feelings. However, once again, I must emphasize that the dress code is vital to perceive and practice appropriately in the HE learning environments. If you have not observed this culture yet, start today, and you will experience the fortune accompanied by appropriate dressing that can make you successful in your learning. There is no regret about proper dressing in the higher education learning environment, and my task is to inform you how to fight isolation by observing and wearing appropriately. Now you know how dressing plays a part in your integration; it is your choice. However, before you put on your costumes daily, think of the questions in the figure.

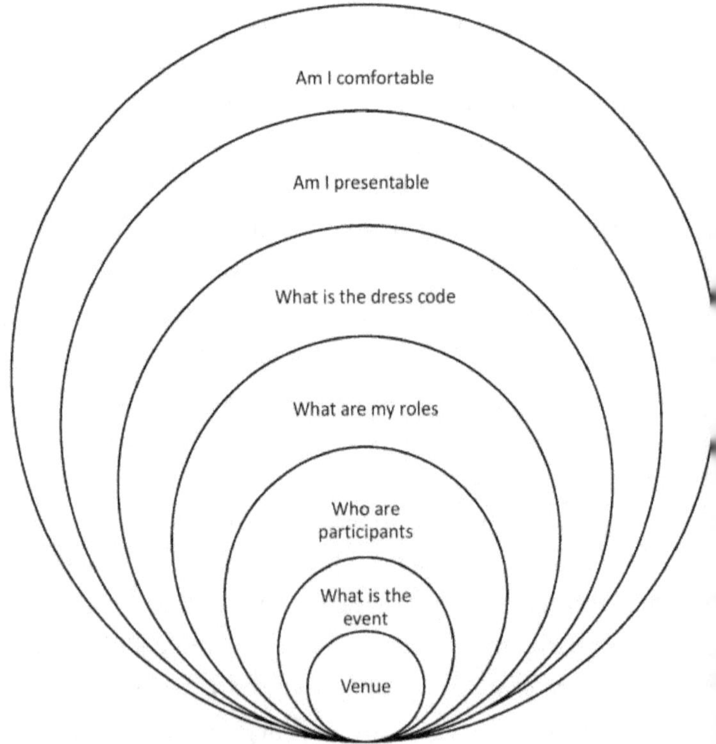

Figure 6. The Questions to Ask When Dressing up

Figure six reminds students of the questions to ask when dressing up for an event. It may be a lecture, seminar, or workshop where the student expects to meet people. Alternatively, the event may be a group study where presentations occur, or the student intends to study individually. Students should be aware of their customers in their learning environment. So, first, the student must be aware of the venue and events she is about to attend. Secondly, knowing the participants and their roles in the activity is essential in selecting appropriate clothing. Thirdly, students must have acquired knowledge of the dress code required and put it on to check its comfort and presentability. Students may ask these basic questions to guide them in selecting an appropriate dress for the day, hours, or minutes.

Chapter 7

Parties and Invitation Practices

*S*ome *parties can be expensive, and others are free of charge. In addition, different cultures demonstrate and celebrate parties in various styles, so higher education students must not transfer their experiences with parties to their learning context without prior investigation.*

Studying in postsecondary institutions involves a lot of ceremonies and parties. Most parties are organized by institution management formally, and some are arranged by students informally. The institution initiates formal parties to celebrate and come together with specific academic or social intentions. Sometimes, the parties are organized for students to socialize with academics and other university staff members. Other times may be for students alone, where they get to know each other, discuss some issues, and even learn from each other in a relaxed mood. Indeed, parties and occasions are vital for students to learn about contextual social culture, including peoples' positions and roles.

Moreover, gatherings such as orientation programs for first-year students are equally important. Most universities inform students of different issues that simplify their stay at university in orientation programs. Depending on the contents and intention, the program may last for hours, days, or weeks. Other ceremonies that gather students are awards, graduations, and other academic rituals and victories. All these events are important, and students who desire to succeed should attend and learn from these events.

The mentioned ceremonies are a few examples of the formal parties held in most tertiary institutions. Sometimes, the gatherings differ from one department to other and institution to another. However, in most cases, academic parties are on the University's calendar and may provide vital information. If students have not investigated the University's ceremonies, reading it now while reviewing this book may be good timing. Read the institution's webpage, learn about official ceremonies and parties, include them in your calendar, and make a reminder on your cell phone. In addition, it might be wise to read the event's intention, content, who is involved, their positions, roles, and influence. Doing that may help you prepare relevant information, including questions about the event.

As mentioned earlier, the institutional management or students may arrange parties. These gatherings can be informal and formal based on the issue students, or officials desire to deal with. For instance, when students invite each other, they do that as it suits them for socialization, enjoyment, or academic purpose. The intention is not to discuss students' educational gathering in this book but social relational issues. So, in this section of ceremonies and part, I will focus only on those associated with social events. These events may be birthday parties, marriage ceremonies, adversaries, and others of a private nature.

Fortunately, there is no way a student will graduate from HE without attending one of these informal parties if he is sociable. Learning in HE involves many actors who may have different issues to celebrate. For instance, students who desire to celebrate birthdays and other life events with others tend to invite their peers, friends, and families. It is always good to have people who can honor the significant memories of your life when you are on a learning journey.

The clothing for informal parties is casual and formal, depending on the nature of the ceremony. Other factors that determine the clothing in a ceremony are the party's purpose, the weather, and the participants. For example, formal celebrations may have different protocols, and students must observe the information on the invitation. For example, the event might be formal if the festival aims at academic events such as signing new publications. Another formal ceremony can be the granting and awarding ceremonies, where some people obtain certificates of excellence, honors, or promotions for academic work or other types of appreciation. Such official parties can also involve other institutional rituals related to fundraising, changing leadership, and the like. Sometimes institutional parties can celebrate donors' and other stakeholders' beliefs and achievements.

The most critical aspect of ceremonies students should observe is identifying whether it is formal or informal. As mentioned earlier, there are formal and informal organized parties within the private traditions, and their protocols may differ significantly. Therefore, understanding the culture of formal (university-organized parties) and private parties (students-organized parties) in the HEIs context is critical and advantageous, especially for students. It may support them in deciding whether to participate, and one must first comprehend the nature of the party and its purpose. The purpose of parties can inform, whether formal or informal and bring insight into the content. The information can support the invitees in accepting or rejecting the invitation based on their needs and the situation.

Another thing that can inform the nature of the ceremony is the persons who called for the party and those invited (students, academics, civilians, friends). Typically, no one informs about other participants unless the party is for a few friends, but you can be a detective to find out. The information can support you in perceiving the party atmosphere, whether you feel comfortable, and if the party will benefit you. You might have known some participants and their behavior to ensure the company you will hang with at the party.

After knowing whether the party is formal or informal and the participants, you may consider the dress code; people usually wear casual party dresses at informal and private parties, depending on the institution's dress code and society's preferences. If you used to wear half-naked to private or informal parties in your previous environment, do not automatically apply it to the new learning environment without investigation. You may be embarrassed if you wear an unacceptable dress because the dress can indeed move people away from you. If you doubt what to wear, you may ask the person who called for the party to inform you of the expected dress code. Dressing style is critical to be confident and comfortable with your outfit in the ceremony.

Cost Sharing in Parties

Some parties can be expensive, and others are free of charge. Different cultures demonstrate and celebrate parties in various styles, so higher education students must not transfer their experiences without prior investigation. For example, it is not always that participation in parties is costless. Sometimes there is a cost-sharing of the expenses associated with parties, whether formal or informal. In most cases, gatherings that involve eating and drinking may be expensive for an individual (invitee) to cover the bill for others.

For this reason, the participants ought to pay for what they expect to consume at the party. Cost-sharing can apply where the host cannot provide free participation, and it may occur between and among students due to the financial limits most students encounter. As a student, you ought to find out how the part you are invited to is organized, especially on the issues of food and drinks. The inquiry is vital to understand whether the party is free of charge or has a share of the party's costs and what exact amount is required. Before committing to the party, you must know its expenses because some parties may be expensive.

Another issue to know in advance is the venue. As mentioned earlier, some parties are institutional, and others are private. Likewise, some parties are held outside the university and others on campus. Non-campus parties may be more expensive than the campus due to expenses associated with venues that must be paid for. So, most off-campus parties are typically arranged based on the cost-sharing scheme, where party participants may obtain food and drink for free and are asked to contribute to the payment of the location or vice versa. Sometimes the participants ought to provide money or bring food and beverages to the communal dining table.

Moreover, on other occasions, participants may be asked to contribute by preparing the party's schedule (making food or cookies collaboratively) or decorating the setting instead of paying for other costs. Therefore, as a student, you may be asked to organize music and other equipment required for the music, such as speakers and singers. Another time you may be part of those who will bring food, utensils, or something else. Even if you are not assigned to contribute, you may find it beneficial to volunteer and be part of the organizers; ask for it.

This culture of cost-sharing is not applicable globally in some cultures; when someone invites you to a party, whether dinner or anything else, the person in question is prepared to pay for your expenses. Such generosity does not apply to all cultures or most tertiary institutions in the West and North. It is difficult for some students to apply their generosity culture to parties, so one should investigate contextual party protocol. If the culture promotes cost-sharing, one should observe it, and vice versa. The misunderstandings related to parties have caused embarrassment to some students. Several stories where students were surprised by invoices related to parties they attended are out there to teach.

Some students have experienced drawbacks concerning parties that have made them unsocial. The experience was unpleasant, but it happened because they were unaware of the contextual learning community party norms. These students came from a different party tradition and were unaware of the requirements of their new learning society. They thought someone else could cover their bills simply because they were invitees. Indeed, it is uncomfortable, and most students find themselves in a strange situation where they should blindly pay for the part they participated in.

Above all, one student, Paul, contended."

"In my culture, if someone invites you for coffee, dinner, a party, or whatever to do with the leisure of eating and drinking, the person will cover all the expenses without question. This thinking lies in the fact that the person who invites you desires to demonstrate his generosity, and it is his ideas, which sometimes may conflict with, your plan, including your budget. We also think the person is seeking and delighted in your company, which is why the invitation. Hence, he is prepared for the cost, and you do not have to bother paying for the expenses. It is more polite that you invite (if you like) the person in the future and show generosity to the person and pay for his expenses."

Paul is not alone in such an ideology of generosity. Some societies have such a culture of invitation where the invitee has nothing to do but show up to the party cheerfully. According to my investigation, most students from benevolent societies may have such perceptions compared to others from other parts of the globe. It does not mean that a non-cost sharing invitation is the only way of demonstrating generosity. It just means that people show generosity differently and in diverse practices. Indeed, calling for a party by itself is a massive sign of kindness from the party organizer, indicating that the host thinks of other people. In turn, everyone who participates in a party demonstrates a kind of generosity, which is vital, especially in the learning environment where time is a limited resource.

Nevertheless, the explanation provided by Paul reminds me of my experiences when I was studying for a bachelor's degree. I liked parties, including meeting new people and learning from them. The first party I attended was an event associated with dinner and dance, to which I was invited by one of my classmates. On the invitation card, she wrote that I had to come with the drinks of my choice and would get food by paying a certain amount. She indicated how grateful she would be to see me at the party. She even suggested that I would have an opportunity to choose a song, and there would be people to sing for me. She informed me that I could even dance for the show if that were appropriate for me. It was a beautiful invitation, although unfamiliar.

A new culture was behind the invitation. It was a lovely invitation but strange because I was unfamiliar with such cost-sharing requests. I came from a culture that resembles Paul's, where no one pays for the food and drinks he consumes at a party he is invited to unless he asks for the invitation. So, I thought a bit; the party would be held at her residence, not in a restaurant, and it would cost nothing. Why does she call for the party if she cannot cook for the guests? Why should I pay for food I do not even know its taste? Why did she invite me if she was not ready to use her time and resources for me? Those were questions I asked without answers due to my previous culture. Maybe you could ask the same questions or even more if you come from a great cultural background as mine, where a guest pays nothing for what he consumes (food and drink) for a visit.

Therefore, the invitation was a challenge, but I desired to participate in the party. I liked meeting people and enjoying and laughing with others on such occasions. Importantly, the idea of singing and dancing trapped and attracted me the most. As the date for the party came closer, I decided to hear from other students. I asked one of my friends, Tasha, if she had received an invitation to the same party and whether she would participate. As indicated in the email, I asked her about the payment culture and whether it was customary for students to receive such an awful invitation to pay for the cost. With positive feelings,

Tasha said she was grateful and excited to receive the invitation and looked forward to participating. She added that it was the students' typical party culture where the attendee shares the costs, and she provided me with details of the benefits of such an arrangement. I appreciated her explanation and clarity about the new invitation and party policy. Her descriptions catalyzed my investigation of contemporary culture, which differed from my previous traditions. In addition, seeing and noting other beneficial social-cultural issues in my learning context was eye-opening. After Tasha's explanation, I started seeing the benefit of cost-sharing for parties and ceremonies.

Advantages of Cost Sharing

Exposure to a new environment may lead to new learning. Based on the explanation I received from Tasha, I realized several reasons for this party's cost-sharing phenomenon. First, we were all students, and no one could afford to pay for someone else party expenses. Second, without one person taking the initiative to invite others, there could be difficult for students to come together. Thirdly, the issue was not the food or drinks but the togetherness and sharing of love, happiness, and other meaningful ideas and feelings. Considering these benefits, I gradually comprehended the reasons behind such a cost-sharing invitation system. Therefore, I went to the party, paid for the food, and shared my joy with other students; it was worth it for me to be there.

I am grateful that I finally got used to the cost-sharing party culture and invitations. Almost every weekend, some parties were held around the University compasses and outside. It was such an experience that it became a learning staff to master as every weekend there were parties. Most students had difficulty choosing which party to attend, but their decisions depended on the budget, the people they desired to associate with, and time. Sometimes we had to pay for everything; the site, food, drinks, and music without ill-feeling because the majority comprehended the meaning behind the party culture. The most important was meeting and exchanging our ideas, being happy, and socializing than eating and drinking separately in the residence or restaurants. Students who comprehended party culture and coped with it experienced joy and were more integrated than others.

Higher education students should remember that it is essential to participate in some parties while undertaking a degree. There are gatherings all over, inside and outside the University's campuses. Gatherings are good tools for fighting isolation in higher education and facilitate students meeting with relevant people. Even if a student has no invitation, she may ask for it because sometimes, the organizers can forget others without ill intentions. So, asking for an invitation to the gathering one desires to attend is not a strange issue. But on the other hand, the forgotten student may think positively and contact the organizer demonstrating her interest.

For example, one may say:

"Hi, I heard there is a party on ... which is very important. If possible, I want to participate in refreshing my mind and meeting new and good people. Am I late to ask for an invitation?

If a student asks politely for participation, the organizer will be motivated to invite the person.

However, you may destroy your opportunity if you blame the organizer for not inviting you and think she is not a good person. Let us say you realize you are not invited to the party but all the other students. Immediately you call the organizer, saying;

"Hi, it is unbelievable that you discriminate against me over all other students. I heard you had invited all students in my cohort except me, and I want to know why. I thought we were friends, but your behavior indicates that you do not want me to participate ...."

Indeed, such a blaming message may scare the organizer and lead to refusing to invite you altogether. Therefore, you need to select sweet words when asking for a favor because it is not your right but a chance to enjoy yourself with peers and friends in a friendly manner. Furthermore, no student with the right to party and ceremony is a privilege provided, or you create for yourself; hence one cannot demand.

Furthermore, if you are unfamiliar, you do not need to participate in a party because you may cause an unnecessary commotion. Some parties create lifelong friendships with people you desire, who can sometimes be from all cultural backgrounds. However, it would help if you were open-minded and courageous enough to attend the invited ceremonies happily. If no one invites you even when you ask for it, you may try to hold a party and invite some peers and others who seem positive. You can even invite those you have been together in the orientation course, group discussions, lectures, and seminars, to start with. It does not mean that one should invite many people for the party to be successful. Even a couple of friends can bring the joy and happiness one needs, not necessarily a crowd. So, as a student, you will be surprised when you take the initiative to invite others; many will take it seriously more than you think.

Another issue is that parties and ceremonies are not held on campus only. Some occur outside the university, mainly if the university accommodates off-campus students. Most off-campus parties happen during the holidays and weekends, and the university management might have no control over them. However, each student should be aware of security for the external parties because most universities are not responsible for students' security outside the university campus. Therefore, be a detective to find adequate information about your safety before attending off-campus parties and blindly engaging in them.

Some students have encountered troubles of different kinds by attending off-campus parties. You can reduce the risk to your safety by associating and participating in parties with reliable friends than alone. Attending external parties requires several preparations and caution that every student must consider before accepting an invitation or organizing the event. It does not mean to scare students, and it does not mean the internal parties are risk-free, but at least the hand of the university is around her students on the campus. The presence of university security guards and the familiar environment for students can increase their safety when they are at parties, contrary to off-campus. However, understanding the risks in the ceremonies may increase valuable knowledge for students' preparation.

Challenges Associated with Parties

There are several issues to consider when students are at a party. First, most parties, especially off-campus, allow the consumption of alcohol and other kinds of stuff. Today, most societies have failed to protect youth from drugs and hazardous drinking and smoking substances. HEIs are not immune to this catastrophe, and most institutions have no control over what students consume at the parties, particularly those held off-campus. In some cases, institutions are not conscious of what students consume in their everyday life either. As a result, there is no control over grocery stores around most university campuses where the university understands what students purchase. So, students buy whatever they desire and from whomever they want.

Most institutions have set aside their responsibility to support students by consuming balanced diets and other essential nutrients. The managements assume that HE students are mature individuals who can care for themselves without help. They often forget that some young adults are directly from high schools, where several rules and regulations support them. And most parents and guardians were available to collaborate with teachers to guide these individuals in almost all areas of their lives. The parents and guardians supported them by becoming their good shepherds in many aspects. For some students, joining a university for a degree is their first experience of departing from their shepherds, hence challenging.

On top of that, some find themselves in a new learning environment with new culture with little or no restriction, protection, and follow-ups. As a result, some struggle to get new shepherds, friends, and reliable people to become their companions. Most of these young men and women are not competent and patient enough to learn about the new environment and people's behavior before associating with them. Instead, they desire to be accepted and included, leading to blindly participating in almost every event. As a result, they associate with people quickly, even when they do not know their behavior, and such action makes them turn away from their learning goals.

Studying in a new environment can bring some challenges, including isolation. It is not always bad to be left alone, but loneliness is not something to applaud. Indeed, some students are not used to being alone, and most fail to tackle loneliness appropriately. They desire to obtain the company of others as quickly as possible and of any nature to avoid loneliness. Sometimes, it does not matter to them what kind of associates they have and their influences; what they need most is somebody to be with and to appreciate. Such desperate students attempt to tie in with people who do not support their learning goals. Unfortunately, they find themselves associating with the wrong people, so the right people do not appear, falling into the hands of those against their learning goals.

Without a doubt, the process of seeking acceptance and acknowledgment from others is challenging. The students used to parental/guardian attention, and protection tend to long for the same treatment from people. The yearning to be part of others and be loved, cared for, and protected forces students to do anything to be part of others. Such students may even forget the good advice they have received from their previous shepherds for years. As a result, they are willing to perform what the new companion asks them in exchange for acceptance and inclusion. The situation may even lead to accepting hazard conditionalities provided to them by such people.

Among the expected conditions most new students receive from those who want to drive them away from their learning goals is to separate them from others. They cage them in one way or another and induce fear that hinders them from contacting others who could guide them better. In some cases, these attention-seeking students may face slavery by obeying the orders of those they desire to be their companions. For instance, some students have engaged in businesses they do not want, such as selling drugs and other stuff for their masters (people they want to hang with). Others have become vulnerable, demonstrating their toughness and ability to entertain by consuming excessive alcohol, smoking, or sexual immoralities. Such students have sacrificed their studies to seek the acceptance and company of others. They do not know it is okay to be left alone.

It is easy for some HE students to get lost, especially those less informed and outside the learning society. These students may originate from different cultural norms from those operating in the institution. They may also have little knowledge of the new learning environment and community than the natives. It may be true that they lack a network and people who can appreciate them. I do not mean that the natives are not affected by searching for a company because some may have come from a different region from the university setting.

However, their situation may differ from international students because they know society better than foreigners and may have no language barriers. Stakeholders, including teachers, parents, and guardians, may sometimes not adequately discuss international students' challenges. As a result, some suffer, and when they do not have anyone to share their challenges with, they drop out. Little is known about the challenges international students encounter in foreign learning environments. Otherwise, if their loved ones would comprehend, some could not allow them to join postsecondary learning environments without proper and adequate guidance about social-relational culture.

The situation is not equal for all students seeking companies. For instance, it might be easier for mature students (people who have job experiences or have been away from their parents and guardians before commencing HE) to resist peer pressure[2]. These adult students may have experienced some related burden that has probably strengthened them more than students from high schools. Likewise, students who are not fully aware of their identity and what they are to others may be drawn by associates away from their learning goals. Indeed, some do not think it is okay to remain alone with destructive associates that kill their dreams and learning objectives.

Instead, as mentioned, they allow other students to define them and even slaver them to obtain a company. Sometimes, such students do whatever their peers tell them, even when they know the actions are illegal, harmful, and against their learning goals.

Yes, back to the party, some parties allow the drinking of alcohol. If you are a consumer of alcohol, make sure you understand your limit. Keep your integrity by not exceeding your level because nothing is more embarrassing at most students' parties than drinking and losing control of your mind and actions. It is NOT OKAY to hear from other students about your activities at parties you are unaware of. Maintain the good intentions of parties, thus, to get together, enjoy the company of each other, and share good moments with others.

Knowing your limit is the essential virtue you must cultivate. If you think you cannot resist alcohol and are weak in controlling your limit, do not attend parties that allow alcohol consumption. Instead, choose non-alcohol parties where you can participate without thinking of losing your mind. Remember, no one has the right to force you to attend parties you do not desire; you ought not to provide a reason behind your absence either; the choice is yours.

I may caution you, though, to make sure you know the content of what you always consume at parties. It might be soft drinks, but knowing its contents and ensuring its safety is vital. Surrounding yourself with sound and trustworthy friends might be better for staying safe. Some students get into trouble when they carelessly leave their drinks without attention. For example, one may go to the bathroom, dance, or attend to their smoking desire outside without caring for their drinks.

Sometimes, a party may accommodate different and unfamiliar people. If the party consists of participants you do not trust, do not leave anything you consume without an attendant. If, for instance, you leave your drink behind with dishonest people, do not drink it in your return. Someone may add some undesirable substances out of your awareness intentionally. Be extra careful when at parties with other students rather than with family members. Enjoy parties consciously and soberly, and care for your friends. Parties can catalyze your integration if you observe my advice and those you have received from the previous and present reliable shepherds.

Undoubtedly, enjoying parties and ceremonies on and off university campuses is good. But, for students, staying focused and safe must be the priority, and the principle should be that if, as a student, you are not sure of your safety at a party or ceremony you desire to attend, avoid it. Likewise, if the party or ceremony endangers your learning goals and life, you should not participate but rather stay aside.

Figure seven indicates the ten commandments for university parties.

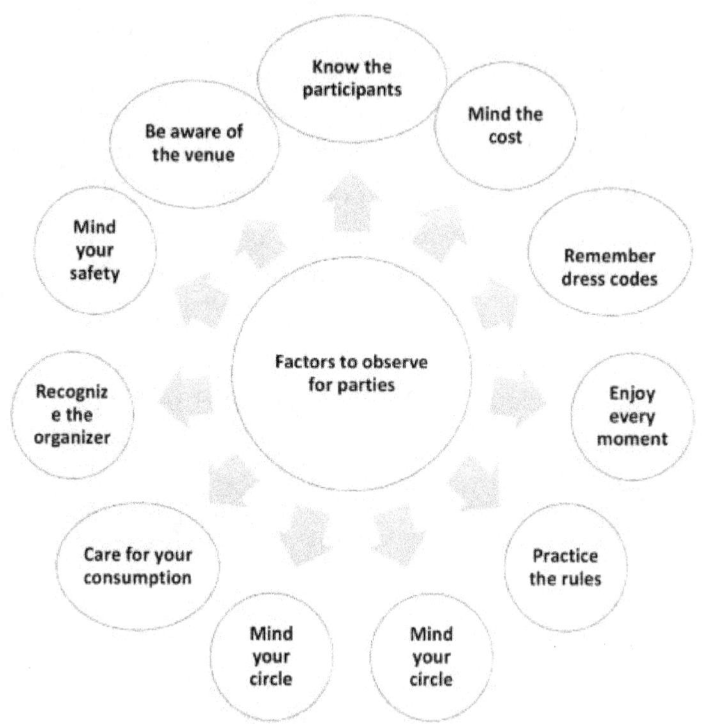

Figure 7. Factors Students Must Observe for Parties

According to Figure seven, higher education students who desire to participate in parties should observe the ten commandments. The first is to mind the cost of the party one desires to attend. Second, as a student, you must find out who the other invitees or participants are to check whether you are comfortable with their company. The third is to know the venue and how to get there on time. Finally, the fourth is to investigate your safety after knowing the venue and other participants.

Further, you must know the organizer(s) and your relationship with the individual(s); no one goes to his enemies' party. Moreover, ensure you know your drink and food consumption limit and their safety in your absence. Again, mind your circle by surrounding yourself with trustworthy people; otherwise, you may risk your life. The eighth commandment is that you must remember the dress code and practice the rules associated with the party, as the ninth commandment. Finally, the tenth commandment in parties, which applies in other areas, is to enjoy every moment. Indeed, students who take notice of these commandments will have unforgettable and remarkable memories of higher education parties.

Conclusion

We have seen scholarly literature inform isolation as one of many reasons that cause student attrition in higher education. But, again, students' isolation is caused by many factors, including students' lack of social-cultural skills that could support them in coping with the contextual social aspects. In addition, a lack of guidance on how students with diverse cultures should adjust to their social learning environment increases the challenge.

Moreover, the current higher education learning environment is multicultural, with stakeholders from different cultural backgrounds who should work together productively. The multicultural situation emerged mainly due to the implementation of globalization and the internationalization policy in higher education. The policies encourage higher education to open across countries and continents' borders where students and academics are mobile, crossing regional borders. As a result, most people from the South and East have joined universities in the West and Northern hemispheres, and vice versa, although there is an imbalance in the openness of borders and movement.

Therefore, the book support readers with basic silly but vital social-relational strategies that may open integration anywhere with anybody. Indeed, several aspects isolate students from the group they wish to be in because of, among others, failure to cope with the cultural codes required. The discussion started with greeting culture, a universal culture found in any society but can bring challenges to strangers if not mastered. Greeting culture becomes meaningful depending on the people involved and the correctness of the practice. Therefore, students should learn and practice appropriate greeting culture accepted in the context for them to succeed.

The author discusses various greetings approaches where some desire to shake hands while others perform different acts such as bending knees or leaning their body forward while greeting. The book mentions the Queens and Pope of the Roman Catholic church as the recipients of greetings style where women bend their knees. In addition, the explanation concerning the disadvantage and advantages of correct performance of greeting actions is discussed to encourage students to be careful. Likewise, the author explains misconceptions about incorrect greetings routines that higher education students should observe, avoid, and learn correctly. Likewise, students should avoid transferring their greeting culture directly to the new learning environment but find the meaning of the new practices to execute the expected greeting style.

Additionally, the discussion turns to the smiling habit, which is common in many societies. However, it is performed differently in most communities and carries various translations. Generally, the author indicates that people smile on different occasions, consciously or unconsciously, and their actions send a message. Though people smile, the author categorizes and translates two smile styles in this book, thus, "I see you" and "I care for you." The difference between these styles is that "I see you" is not necessarily accompanied by greetings or conversation, while "I care for you" does. The book guides students and other readers to practice the smiling act most acceptable in their context and take precautions in their translations.

Furthermore, the book analyses the advantages and disadvantages of smiling behavior and the confusion the action can cause people unfamiliar with the two natures of smiling acts. The author mentioned the scientific benefits of smiling and how the smile can bring fortune and break impossibilities. Therefore, Elizabeth emphasizes selecting the contextual correct style and performance to avoid misunderstandings and confusion. Likewise, the author provides her experience with smiling and others to motivate students to learn the proper smiling techniques and practice.

Another social-cultural issue explained in this book is the dress code. Higher education institutions have no uniforms unless the institution is unique for specific folks. Therefore, students should observe the dominant contextual dressing style in different events and not necessarily their previous cultural outfit if they want to be part of the learning community. Remember that the author supports students with strategies to avoid isolation, so costumes may lead to the integration and acceptance most students desire.

Besides, the author demonstrates how the dress can talk more about the students than how they verbally explain themselves. So, students should wear according to the occasion, and one may require a specific dressing style for each event. Sometimes, proper dressing may be translated differently based on the circumstances and contextual dressing translation culture. However, students are encouraged to wear what they feel comfortable and contextually acceptable to the event.

Indeed, the message in this book reminds the readers of different dress codes that may be part of one's identity or the organization they represent. Furthermore, the discussion underlined that violating the dress codes of an organized institution might lead to diverse consequences for the individual, including withdrawing from membership.

Further, Elizabeth encourages students to seek information about the dress codes of their institutions and look smart while avoiding out-of-context outfits. Although most universities do not tell their students the dress required before their enrolment, students must be detectives to understand the requirements before or soon after admission.

However, it is not forbidden for students to dress anyhow, but it may lead to disadvantages concerning integration and inclusion. Besides, students can express their culture and integrate it into contextual cultures where appropriate. Nevertheless, people may be scared to involve conservative students not interested in others' cultures. Such students may sometimes not be allowed to represent the institution if they find their dressing style does not conform with those they represent, it may be biased, but it happens. The author mentions the experiences some students have had concerning their outfits, where they had to incur the cost of buying new outfits. Therefore, although it is a personal choice, proper dressing can be a gateway to many fortunes. Most importantly, every student should consider positive contextual aspects of dressing that bring advantages, not disadvantages.

Consequently, the author discusses social-cultural aspects that involve parties. She informs the need for students to participate in different social events in and out of the institutions' compounds for their integration. Thus, it might be academic meetings accompanied by the festival, private birthday parties, or others. Normally, students participate in various parties where they meet people who may encourage or discourage them from focusing on their learning objectives.

Unfortunately, not all students obtain productive companions who can support them in focusing on their learning goals. Some fall into the hands of masters who turn them into enslaved people and sometimes kill their dreams and learning objectives. Nevertheless, most students obtain associates who are genuine and supportive through parties. Therefore, students should carefully select the parties to attend based on other participants' intentions.

Nevertheless, the book discusses cultural differences in holding parties. The author mentions parties where cost-sharing is a protocol for some university students and new culture for others. Elizabeth discusses the reasons for such an arrangement for cost-sharing and how it can catalyze students' gatherings. The author indicates that a cost-sharing system of organizing parties may benefit students socializing as they increase gathering frequency. Also, students contribute to the event, where it becomes less expensive for all, and the situation encourages them to participate. However, the cost-sharing rule does not apply globally, so students must investigate the contextual party norms and practice them accordingly.

The book emphasizes safety and companionship at parties, especially those held off-campus. Not all students reside in-campus due to the limited space some universities have and the rapid increase in student population. So, where students are, parties follow them; hence, off-campus parties for students are familiar in some universities. So, the author advises students to be extra careful participating in such ceremonies off campus because the universities, in most cases, are not responsible for their safety. Thus, students must choose the party to attend and accompany by reliable and trustworthy friends.

Equally important, students must care for their consumption and be with people they trust to avoid traps that their negligence may cause. Today students are the source of many businesses, legal and illegal. Some find it easy to sell whatever they desire to students, and universities have no control of the market around their campuses. Therefore, parties may be one source of illegal business for drugs and excessive alcohol to students. The author argues that students should be careful about what they consume at parties and not leave their drinks and food with people they do not trust.

Although the book discusses only four significant social-cultural aspects, one may find many cultural relational issues students should observe in their context to succeed. The author intends that all higher education students correctly evaluate, learn, and practice the necessary contextual social culture while integrating with others in the learning environment. The discussed cultural elements in this book are fundamental for anyone willing to create contact with others. Although the author emphasizes students' contextual social culture as a determinant of their practices, the aim is not to assimilate students but to help them comprehend and perform the acceptable social norms that facilitate their integration. Indeed, exercising contextual cultural norms while integrating with previously acquired ones is beneficial.

Undoubtedly, no one is forcing students to be part of the new learning community, but there are several benefits to becoming one. The book highlights silly and vital social-relational challenges and proposes strategies to solve them. It also informs of misunderstandings when meeting new cultures and the techniques to appropriately associate with others in a new environment.

The book can benefit people outside academia, and it is up to the readers to pick relevant practical social-relational proposals based on their context. However, greeting and smiling at people is vital in any society, and dressing appropriate may attract and create relevant associates. Furthermore, we are social beings, so parties get people together and create relationships that may last for a lifetime. Therefore, learning the correct social-relational contextual culture and practicing it correctly in the learning environment is beneficial and a weapon for isolation.

Now you know, I have told you the most. Information is Power.

References

Ali, A., Kohun, F., & Levy, Y. (2007). Dealing with social isolation to minimize doctoral attrition- A Four Stage Framework. International Journal of Doctoral Studies, 2(1), 33-49.

Becker, F., & Becker, S. (2008). Young adult carers in the UK. Experiences, needs, and services for carers aged 16-24.

Beer, C., & Lawson, C. (2018). Framing attrition in higher education: A complex problem. Journal of Further and Higher Education, 42(4), 497-508.

Carter, S., & Kumar, V. (2017). 'Ignoring me is part of learning': Supervisory feedback on doctoral writing. Innovations in Education and Teaching International, 54 (1), 68-75.

Gabb, R., Milne, L., & Cao, L. (2006). Understanding attrition and improving transition. A Review.

Golde, C. M. (2000). Should I stay or should I go? Student descriptions of the doctoral attrition process. The review of higher education, 23(2), 199-227.

Golde, C. M. (2005). The role of the department and discipline in doctoral student attrition: Lessons from four departments. The Journal of Higher Education, 76(6), 669-700.

Grant, B. M. (2005). Fighting for space in supervision: Fantasies, fairytales, fictions, and fallacies. International Journal of Qualitative Studies in Education, 18 (3), 337-354. doi:10.1080/09518390500082483.

Johnes, G., & McNabb, R. (2004). Never give up on the good times: student attrition in the UK. Oxford Bulletin of Economics and Statistics, 66 (1), 23-47.

Kettell, L. (2020). Young adult carers in higher education: the motivations, barriers, and challenges involved–a UK study. Journal of Further and Higher Education, 44(1), 100-112.

Maher, M., & Macallister, H. (2013). Retention and attrition of students in higher education: Challenges in modern times to what works. Higher Education Studies, 3(2), 62-73. doi:10.5539/hes.v3n2p62

Manathunga, C. (2005). The development of research supervision: "Turning the light on a private space." International Journal for Academic Development, 10(1), 17-30.

Manathunga, C. (2007). Supervision as mentoring: The role of power and boundary-crossing. Studies in Continuing education, 29(2), 207-221.

Manathunga, C. (2009). Research as an intercultural 'contact zone.' Discourse: Studies in the Cultural Politics of Education, 30(2), 165-177.

Manathunga, C. (2014). Intercultural postgraduate supervision: Reimagining time, place and knowledge. Routledge.

Mayo, D. T., Helms, M. M., & Codjoe, H. M. (2004). Reasons to remain in college: A comparison of high school and college students. International Journal of Educational Management.

McMillan, J. (2005). Course change and attrition from higher education. Australian Council for Educational Research (ACER). LSAY Research Reports, 43.

O'Keeffe, P. (2013). A sense of belonging: Improving student retention. College Student Journal, 47(4), 605-613.

Sempik, J., and S. Becker. (2013). Young Adult Carers at School: Experiences and Perceptions of Caring and Education. London: Carers Trust.

Sempik, J., and S. Becker. (2014). Young Adult Carers at College and University. London: Carers Trust.

Tinto, V. (1987). Leaving college: Rethinking the causes and cures of student attrition. ERIC.

Urassa, E. P. (2021). The Cultural Qualities you Must Acquire to Succeed in Higher Education. Xlibris Publisher, USA.

Wisker, G. (2005). The good supervisor: Supervising postgraduate and undergraduate research for doctoral theses and dissertations. New York: Macmillan.

Index

A

D

J

K

L

Printed and bound by Information is Power, Oslo, Norway, with support from Draft2digital.

[1] ACCORDING TO BECKER and Becker (2008), young adult are students aged 16 to 24.

[2] It is a force and desires to perform similar activities and even attend social events where others of the same courses, degree, department, discipline, and institution participate.

Did you love *Simple and Silly Social -Cultural Strategies to Fight Isolation in Higher Education*? Then you should read *Articulating Research Students' Relational and Social Expectations*[1] by Elizabeth Paradiso Urassa!

**Articulating Research Students'
Relational

and Social Expectations**

Elizabeth Paradiso Urassa

2

Student attrition is a persisting challenge that scholars have discussed for years. The problem affects higher education institutions worldwide, regardless of structure (full-time, part-time), levels (doctoral, master, and bachelor's degrees), and resource availability. Although many issues contribute to the problem, the student's social-relational aspects are the leading causes. So, without constructive and understandable

---

1. https://books2read.com/u/bxJ0D6

2. https://books2read.com/u/bxJ0D6

communication, students and supervisors cannot collaborate. Student attrition is a problem caused mainly by the failure of supervision partners to communicate their needs and expectations. Therefore, the book will help research students and their learning agencies to comprehend their social relational needs and expectations and how to fulfill them.

About the Author

Elizabeth is a former teacher, school inspector, and job advisor. During her Ph.D. study, she recognized students and their learning agency encounter with supervision. Since then, her primary responsibilities have been supporting people, including students and supervisors in higher education, with information and strategies to overcome diverse challenges, including isolation.